WRITING
EFFICIENT
PROGRAMS

PRENTICE-HALL SOFTWARE SERIES
Brian W. Kernighan, advisor

WRITING
EFFICIENT
PROGRAMS

Jon Louis Bentley

Department of Computer Science
Carnegie-Mellon University
Pittsburgh, Pennsylvania 15213

PRENTICE-HALL, INC., Englewood Cliffs, New Jersey 07632

Library of Congress Cataloging in Publication Data

Bentley, Jon Louis. (date)
  Writing efficient programs.

  (Prentice-Hall software series)
  Includes bibliographical references and
index.
  1. Electronic digital computers—Programming.
I. Title. II. Series.
QA76.6.B455   001.64′2   82-555
ISBN 0-13-970251-2   AACR2
ISBN 0-13-970244-X (pbk.)

Editorial/Production Supervision: *Lynn S. Frankel*
Paper Cover Design: *Ray Lundgren*
Case Cover Design: *Adapted by Anne T. Bonanno*
Manufacturing Buyer: *Gordon Osbourne*

This book was set in Times Roman by *Fast* on a Mergenthaler Omnitech®/2000
photo-typesetter driven by the Scribe® document production system.

Printed in the United States of America

10

ISBN 0-13-970251-2
ISBN 0-13-970244-X {pbk.}

PRENTICE-HALL INTERNATIONAL, INC., *London*
PRENTICE-HALL OF AUSTRALIA PTY. LIMITED, *Sydney*
PRENTICE-HALL OF CANADA, LTD., *Toronto*
PRENTICE-HALL OF INDIA PRIVATE LIMITED, *New Delhi*
PRENTICE-HALL OF JAPAN, INC., *Tokyo*
PRENTICE-HALL OF SOUTHEAST ASIA PTE. LTD., *Singapore*
WHITEHALL BOOKS LIMITED, *Wellington, New Zealand*

To my brother,
Jay Robert Bentley,
1958-1980

CONTENTS

Appendix D   **The Pascal Dialect**   **152**

                 References   **159**

                 Index   **167**

PREFACE

THE PROBLEM AND THE SOLUTION

The primary task of software engineers is the cost-effective development of maintainable and useful software. There are many secondary problems lurking in that definition. One such problem arises from the term "useful": to be useful in the application at hand, software must often be efficient (that is, use little time or space). The problem we will consider in this book is building efficient software systems.

There are a number of levels at which we may confront the problem of efficiency. These are defined in Section 1.2 and include the overall system design, the program's algorithms and data structures, the translation to machine code, and the underlying system software and hardware; many books discuss efficiency at each of those levels. In this book we will investigate efficiency at a design level that is practiced by many but discussed by few. This level is called "writing efficient code" and can be defined as follows:

> The activity of writing efficient code takes as input a high-level language program (which incorporates efficient algorithms and data structures) and produces as output a program in the same high-level language that is suitable for compilation into efficient machine code. The operations undertaken at this level are beneath most work on algorithms and data structures yet are too complex for most current and foreseeable compilers.

An example of this activity can be found in Chapter 2, where we will increase the speed of a particular program by a factor of almost seven. In later chapters we will study a set of twenty-six rules that can be used to increase the efficiency of software systems by factors that vary from a few percent to orders of magnitude. These rules can easily be misused, so an important part of the book is emphasizing exactly when one should (and should not) use the rules.

HACKING OR ENGINEERING?

The rules that we will study increase efficiency by making changes to a program that often decrease program clarity, modularity, and robustness. When this coding style is applied indiscriminately throughout a large system (as it often has been), it usually increases efficiency slightly but leads to late software that is full of bugs and impossible to maintain. For these reasons, techniques at this level have earned the name of "hacks". It is hard to argue with this criticism; although solid work has been done in this domain, much work at this level is pure and simple hacking in the most pejorative sense of that term.

But writing efficient code need not remain the domain of hackers. The purpose of this book is to present work at this level as a set of engineering techniques. The following are some of the differences between hacks and engineering techniques:

- Hacks are applied indiscriminately; engineering techniques are applied in a well-defined context. While the medicine man peddles snake oil on the street, the physician treats a patient only in a well-defined relationship. The extreme measures of the surgeon are taken in a well-staffed and well-equipped hospital, and only when the patient needs surgery.
- Hacks are described loosely and informally; engineering techniques are described precisely.
- Hacks are created after a moment's thought; engineering techniques are firmly based on scientific principles and are well tested in both laboratory and applied contexts.
- Hacks are passed on by word of mouth, at best; engineering techniques are described in a common literature and are referred to by name when applied.
- Hacks are described out of context; engineering techniques are presented with indicators and contra-indicators for their application.
- Hacks are applied without certainty; engineering techniques can be tested for their appropriateness and effectiveness.

The tools that we will study are presented as engineering techniques and not as hacks.

So how do the techniques of this book relate to the established engineering techniques that go by the name of "structured programming"? At first glance the two approaches might appear to be contradictory: structured programming emphasizes structure almost to the exclusion of efficiency, while the techniques we will study emphasize efficiency that at times flies in the face of program structure. Deeper investigation, though, shows not only that the two viewpoints can peacefully coexist, but that they are in fact mutually supporting. Structured programming provides a basis for the efficiency techniques: we use structured programming to achieve a correct (but possibly inefficient) program that we then improve with these techniques, and we use methods of structured programming as we apply the efficiency techniques to ensure that we preserve correctness. The efficiency techniques also support structured programming: their existence allows us to ignore microscopic efficiency issues in the first versions of programs (knowing that we can later eliminate any inefficiencies that matter), and to concentrate on the more important problem of building a correct and maintainable system.

USING THE BOOK

In writing this book I have tried to follow the example of McNair [1972], who wrote the following in the Preface of his surgery book.

> This book is not intended, nor has it ever been, for the well-trained young surgeon working in a well-equipped modern hospital, with a well-stocked library at hand for reference and an experienced senior colleague available to give advice. Rather it is written to help the less experienced surgeon working, often alone, under conditions that may be far from ideal, who is expected to possess a far wider knowledge of medicine than is the modern specialist.... [Contributors] have given priority to practical advice and have avoided excessive academic detail.

This book is not intended as a scholarly treatise on esoteric aspects of computer science. Rather, its purpose is to give practicing programmers both a mind-set and some practical tools to help them make their programs more efficient.

The primary reader for whom this book is intended is a professional programmer who works on a team that designs, develops and maintains software products. This book assumes that context; programmers working on more limited projects can ignore discussions about the issues that arise in broader environments. Most programmers should be able to read most of this book in several hours of careful study; over sixty programmers at Bell Telephone Laboratories and at IBM have read preliminary versions of this book as a pre-course assignment, and almost all of them got through most of the book within that time. The most important use of this book will be as a reference: the division of Chapters 4 and 5 into sections, the summary in Appendix C, and the Index are all designed to help the programmer find the technique applicable to the problem at hand. The techniques we will study have been applied to increase the efficiency of many software systems; "war stories" about such applications can be found throughout the book.

This book has been used to teach several classes in industrial settings. It was the basis of an eight-lecture-hour course entitled "Building Efficient

Programs" at Bell Telephone Laboratories in Columbus, Ohio. The students in that course had completed a series of courses including Data Structures and Algorithms, Program Verification, Compiler Theory, and Software Engineering; the purpose of the course was to integrate the previous material by considering the problem of efficiency in software systems. The students read the entire book, and lectures were primarily on this material, but I felt free to use material from the previous courses. In a Program Verification course for IBM's Information Systems Division the students were required to read Chapters 1 and 3 and Section 5.1; the remainder of the book was optional (many of the students read it). The book served as a source of examples for programs to verify, and as a bridge between the programming-in-the-small of the course and the programming-in-the-large the students did on their jobs. The book is the basis of a one-hour seminar in which over a thousand industrial programmers have participated; one hour is enough to survey the example of Chapter 2, the methodology of Chapter 3, and several rules from Chapters 4 and 5.

Another reader for whom this book is intended is the computer hobbyist. Because of the slow speeds of many personal computers, efficiency is more important on hobbyist systems than on most computers used by professional programmers. Most hobbyists should be able to read all of this book (though it may take them longer than the professional programmer); the only skill it assumes is a reading knowledge of a high-level computer language such as Pascal. I would like to make one heart-felt appeal to the hobbyist reading this book: although you might think that the problems of working on big software teams (such as writing clean, well-documented code) are not relevant to you, heed the warnings about them anyway. The next time you have to look at a program several months after you wrote it, you'll be glad you did.

A point of concern to some hobbyists and professionals might be the fact that the programs in this book are written in a dialect of the Pascal language. Although that language is gaining popularity among both hobbyists and professionals, it is not yet the *lingua franca* that it is in universities. The examples in the book do not exploit any peculiarities of Pascal, and readers familiar with any high-level language should be able to read all of the programs. For the reader unfamiliar with Pascal, Appendix D includes both a complete (small) Pascal program, and a glossary of Pascal constructs used in the book.

This book can also be used in college courses in computer science. It is not appropriate as a primary text for a semester course, but it could be used as a supplemental text in any of the following courses:

- **Algorithms and Data Structures.** Many texts on algorithms and data structures emphasize "big-oh" analyses of program performance and ignore entirely the constant factors hidden in those analyses. That bent is productive for many purposes, but it can be deceptive when one is concerned with implementing an efficient program. For instance, in Section 8.2 we will study a binary search program from the excellent algorithms text of Aho, Hopcroft, and Ullman [1974]; applying the techniques of this book to a simple Pascal implementation of their program increases its speed by a factor of over fifty. I have used this book as a supplemental text in a one-semester, senior-level course on "Applied Algorithm Design" at Carnegie-Mellon University, together with a standard primary text. This approach combines the best of both worlds: asymptotic analysis keeps the student's head in the clouds, while attention to implementation details keeps his feet on the ground.

- **Software Engineering.** This book addresses the general problem of efficiency in software systems. Although it concentrates on a particular approach, it mentions and uses tools at other design levels. It could therefore form the basis for a series of from three to six one-hour lectures on efficiency in a Software Engineering course.

- **Systems Programming.** Efficiency is crucial in operating systems and in most compilers. Since algorithms for most tasks in those contexts are now well-established, much of the efficiency to be gained comes from the techniques of this book. This book could also be used in a compiler course to stimulate thought on the relative importance of various approaches to efficiency.

- **A Seminar on Programming-In-The-Small.** The programs in this book are motivated by pragmatic considerations, yet many exhibit subtle mathematical reasoning about programs. This book could therefore be used for several weeks of study in a course on Programming Methodologies or Program Verification.

An important caveat in teaching this material in colleges is that programmers must have a great deal of maturity and experience before they can appreciate when these efficiency tools should be applied. I would therefore recommend that these techniques be taught only to students who have worked on at least one large program (by college standards; say, at least 1000 lines of code).

Each chapter of this book includes a set of exercises (no research problems are in those sets). Many of the exercises could require either ten minutes or ten hours, depending on the scope of the answer. A classroom instructor who assigns exercises should therefore be very careful to tell the class exactly what level of detail is appropriate for each problem.

ACKNOWLEDGMENTS

The content of this book has benefitted greatly from the extensive contributions of several dozen individuals; limitations of space on paper and in my head prohibit me from listing them all, so a communal thank-you will have to suffice. Particularly insightful were the careful comments of Al Aho, Peter Deutsch, Cynthia Hibbard, Steve Johnson, Brian Kernighan, Bruce Leverett, Ed McCreight, John McDermott, Doug McIlroy, Al Newell, Joe Newcomer, Bob

Sproull, Don Stanat, Guy Steele, Chris Van Wyk and Bill Wulf. Invaluable
help was provided by Bob Chansler, John Majernik, Elaine Rich, Guy Steele,
Bill Trosky and Bill Wulf, who wrote programs for various computer systems.
The discerning eyes of professional programmers at Bell Telephone Laboratories
and IBM saw many weaknesses in preliminary versions missed by my academic
friends; I thank all of those students for teaching me so much. Bob Michaud of
IBM and Cary Strohecker and Win Wilhoyte of Bell all worked very hard to
make sure that teaching in their companies was a pleasant learning experience for
me. The research underlying portions of this work was supported in part by the
Office of Naval Research under Contract N00014-76-C-0370, and encouraged by
Dick Lau of that office.

Manipulating the form of this book was made almost painless by several
document production programs at Carnegie-Mellon, the most important of which
is Reid's [1980] document specification language and compiler, Scribe. The
few rough spots I found in using that tool were immediately smoothed over by
the staff of Unilogic, Ltd. (which maintains Scribe). Ed Frank designed the
book format and used Scribe to produce the final camera-ready copy in that format. His work turned a task that is months of agony for most authors into a few
question sessions for me. I am especially indebted to Margie Ast for her contributions far above and beyond those dictated by her job as secretary. Not only
did she enter the manuscript and then edit most of it several times, she found
and corrected hundreds of minor bugs and made many suggestions that improved
the final product.

Pittsburgh, Pennsylvania   J. L. B.
March, 1982

WRITING
EFFICIENT
PROGRAMS

1

INTRODUCTION

This book is about an approach to building efficient computer systems called "writing efficient code". To put the approach in context, we will consider the importance of efficiency in Section 1.1 and study avenues to efficiency in Section 1.2. Section 1.3 is an overview of the book, and Section 1.4 then briefly surveys previous work on the problem of writing efficient code.

1.1 THE IMPORTANCE OF EFFICIENCY

Programmers' views on the importance of efficiency underwent a radical change in the early 1970's. In the 1950's and 1960's programmers worked on small, slow machines; reputable programming texts taught tricks that saved a byte here and a memory cycle there, but often obscured the purpose of the program. In the 1970's the costs of machines decreased while their performance increased, the size of software systems grew, and suddenly the dominant cost of most systems was not the cost of hardware but rather the effort required to develop and maintain software. Whereas the texts of the 1960's emphasized efficiency to the exclusion of program structure, the texts of the 1970's emphasized structure to the exclusion of efficiency.[1] Thus we have seen the pendulum swing from one extreme to another in just a few years, and we have to ask where it will come to rest.

On the one hand, there is substantial evidence for the importance of structure. Programming costs are huge and methodologies for producing structured code demonstrably reduce both development and maintenance costs (see, for instance, Brooks [1975, Chapter 8]). Although these methodologies might be slightly detrimental to the efficiency of the systems, they are well worth the price. The efficiency of many systems is unimportant because the programs are run on fast machines with large memories, but the development costs of any large system are always large and are therefore always important. These arguments firmly establish the importance of methodologies for producing correct and maintainable code.

On the other hand, we cannot ignore efficiency; inefficiency can make some systems useless. Brooks [1975, Chapter 9] reports that the first version of the IBM FORTRAN H compiler, on a System/360 Model 65 with drums, compiled programs at the rate of only five cards per minute. Few users would have spent the sixteen hours and thousands of dollars required to compile a five-thousand line program. Less extreme examples of inefficiency are often as intolerable: if a real-time system for recording long-distance telephone bills handled 98% of all calls correctly but failed to record the two percent of the calls when heavy traffic taxed its performance capability, that could cost a telephone

---

[1]As an example of the prevalent attitude from the 1960's, Neuhold and Lawson [1971, p. 41] offer the following advice early in their PL/I programming text.

> The use of constants in a program is another point of concern. We specified in some of our previous examples calculations that involve only constants (e.g., 1/2, 2**3). If such a calculation appears in a loop, it represents, in general, a bad programming technique. To get higher execution speed, it is much better to insert the result of the calculation when the program is constructed (e.g., 0.5 for 1/2 and 8 for 2**3).

Similar hints are given to the student elsewhere in their text. Five years later in their PL/I text, Conway and Gries [1976, p. 179] explicitly ignore optimizations at this level in statements like the following:

> [I]f your sorting program is particularly efficient it is because you devised a clever plan [i.e., algorithm], and not because a mediocre plan was cleverly described in PL/I statements.

McCracken [1957, p. 81] had a more balanced attitude about changes at this level.

> These choices illustrate a point which we shall see recurring: there is almost always a choice between memory space, machine time, and programming time. In this case, we could reduce the machine time at the expense of a slightly longer program and more time spent on analyzing and coding. In many cases when a code is being written, savings and refinements become obvious which would require rewriting the code. Quick analysis of the time and space requirements, however, may show that the advantages are overshadowed by the cost of reprogramming, and the code is left as is. In other cases the program being written may be used for hundreds of hours, making it worthwhile to spend much time in reducing the time to a minimum.

system millions of dollars per year. Efficiency becomes more important with the increasing popularity of microcomputers; many programmers are returning to the old days of 64K bytes of memory and cycle times of dozens of microseconds. In all of these contexts, a methodology that produces an inefficient system cannot be used. Vyssotsky [1976] was able to argue the above case in more concrete terms by describing efficiency problems in the Bell System.

> It's popular these days to say that computer hardware is so cheap that you don't really need to worry much about how fast programs run, because programmers cost more than machine time.... I have an application in field trial now where, unless we find a smarter way of looking at it, we could have to spend as much as $200,000,000 on commercial computer hardware to deploy this one application.... I'm told that the total cost of ESS [Electronic Switching Systems] hardware deployed so far is about four billion dollars. Most of this cost is for machines which run one of only two different operational programs. Viewed in this light, cost and performance do matter.

Even if a system is efficient enough to meet its performance specifications, a ten-percent increase in speed can decrease the cost of each run by that amount, and those savings can quickly add up.

To summarize this section, we should take with us the following two facts in our investigation of efficiency in computer systems:

- The development and maintainability of a software system are always crucial; techniques that ease those tasks *must* be employed.
- Efficiency plays a crucial role in some systems; in those cases we cannot ignore efficiency.

1.2 DESIGN LEVELS

In the previous section we considered the importance of efficiency: it is one of many issues to be considered in the overall life of a computer system. In this section we will consider the next natural question: when we do need to make a system efficient, where is that efficiency to be gotten? In most systems there are a number of design levels at which we can increase efficiency, and we should work at the proper level to avoid being penny-wise and pound-foolish. The following list of design levels in computer systems is inspired by a similar list given by Reddy and Newell [1977]; for each level we will consider the design activity that goes on and the possibilities for speedups at that level.

1. **System Structure.** The overall system structure is the decomposition of the system into modules; this is the highest-level decision in the design hierarchy. This level is crucial for efficiency; with some system structures it is impossible to achieve an efficient system, no matter how efficient the implementation, while with other system structures it is hard *not* to achieve

an efficient system. Unfortunately, efficiency is rarely considered early in the design process, and many high-level designs are implemented even though they are doomed to failure from their conception. Smith [1980, 1981] has developed a methodology that allows a system designer to predict the efficiency of the implementation of a high-level design from the design itself. That methodology can play an important role in achieving efficient systems.

An important design task at this level is problem specification. For instance, if we are designing a compiler and insist that it must produce the best object code possible, then theoretical results tell us that the problem cannot be solved; on the other hand, if we merely ask that the compiler produce "good" object code (where "good" must be precisely defined), then that is well within the bounds of current technology.

2. **Intramodular Structure.** Given the decomposition of the overall system into modules, the next task is the design of each module. There are two related considerations in the design of a module: the *data structure* with which the module represents the information it contains and the *algorithms* that operate on that data. The choice of data structures within a module often has a profound effect on the efficiency of the overall system. Sophisticated algorithms are applicable less often, but when they can be brought to bear they yield substantial results. References to texts on algorithms and data structures can be found in Section 3.2.

3. **Writing Efficient Code.** The activity of writing efficient code takes as input a high-level language program (which incorporates efficient algorithms and data structures) and produces as output a program in the same high-level language that is suitable for compilation into efficient machine code. The operations undertaken at this level are beneath most work on algorithms and data structures yet are too complex for most current and foreseeable compilers. We will see in Chapters 2 through 5 a number of techniques for writing efficient code that are almost independent of the particular system on which the program is to be implemented; they yield the same speedups (usually a factor of between two and ten) across a wide variety of systems. In Chapter 6 we will study techniques that are applicable only in particular systems but can often squeeze another factor of two or more out of the run time.

4. **Translation to Machine Code.** A high-level specification of an efficient computation must be translated to the language of the target machine before it can be executed. This step should usually be accomplished by a compiler. Statistics show that programmers are more productive in high-level languages (see Brooks [1975, Chapter 8]), and good compilers can produce code that is as good as that produced by experienced assembly coders (see Wulf *et al* [1975]). For a general discussion of the principles underlying optimizing compilers, see Aho and Ullman [1977],

Schaeffer [1975], or Waite [1974]; Shaw and Wulf [1980] study the impact of language design decisions on the speed of compiled programs. In some systems it is effective to produce object code by having a programmer write in the assembly code of the object machine; we will consider this further in Section 3.2 and study an example in Appendix B.

5. **System Software.** Most programs are executed under an operating system (or run-time system) that provides services for the user programs but also introduces overhead costs. Those costs can be reduced in two ways. The first way is to fine-tune each operation in the system (often using the techniques of writing efficient code); Nelson [1981] does exactly that to reduce the cost of a remote procedure call by a factor of over thirty. The second way to reduce operating system overhead is by careful scheduling of the shared resources. As an example of this approach, Fuller and Baskett [1975] study the effect of various paging and scheduling policies on the throughput achieved for a drum storage device. Sauer and Chandy's [1981] text covers in detail the mathematical basis of performance improvements at this design level, and surveys several applications of this approach.

6. **Hardware.** Brooks [1975, Chapter 4] describes a trichotomy due to Blaauw that identifies three levels of a hardware computing system. The *architecture* is the user's view of the system (usually given in the assembly language programming manual), the *implementation* is the structure of the device that implements the architecture, and the *realization* embodies the implementation in a particular technology. Efficiency improvements can be achieved at each of these levels. The architecture can be specialized to a certain task to decrease code size or increase speed (or both). The implementation can be tailored to increase performance for greater cost (by increased parallelism, for instance). Finally, performance can often be attained by using faster and more expensive device technologies in a realization.

There are two important implications of this hierarchy of design levels. The more spectacular implication has been persuasively defended by Reddy and Newell [1977]. They argue that in certain systems, the speedups that one can achieve at each of these levels can be multiplied to increase the performance of a system by a factor of a million. This is only possible in hierarchical systems with the property that speedups at one design level do not preclude speedups at other levels, and usually requires several man-years of effort to achieve. Reddy and Newell give several levels in their hierarchy that are not mentioned above (such as knowledge sources and heuristics, which are applicable primarily to Artificial Intelligence domains), and give examples of speedups achieved at each of the levels.

The above design levels are important even if we are attempting more modest speedups—say, of "only" a factor of ten. Reddy and Newell's examples show that it is often possible to achieve factors of ten to twenty at any one of the six levels in the above list. Thus it is often sufficient to work at only one level to achieve the efficiency desired in the system. A programmer must be careful to choose the correct level at which to work; it might be easy to speed up the system software by a factor of ten and almost impossible to speed up the hardware by a similar factor, or vice versa.

Throughout the rest of this book we will concentrate on the design level of writing efficient code; as we do so, we must remember that there are often substantial benefits to be had at other levels. We will return to this issue in detail in Chapters 3, 7 and 8.

1.3 AN OVERVIEW OF THE BOOK

Practitioners have long worked at the level of writing efficient code, yet there is little written about the subject in most discussions of efficiency in software systems. The purpose of this book is to describe this activity to software engineers concerned with efficiency.

In Chapter 2 we will study the activity in its application to a subroutine that arose in a real system; by manipulating the Pascal source code we can decrease the procedure's run time by a factor of almost seven. Careful (but not clever) hand translation of the resulting Pascal program into IBM System/360-370 assembly code results in a program that is over seventeen times faster than the code a typical compiler produced from the original Pascal program. The purpose of this chapter is not to explore tricks either in Pascal or on the IBM System/360-370; rather, those languages are used to illustrate many of the general techniques we will investigate later and to study the interaction writing efficient code and efficient assembly coding.

Although the techniques of writing efficient code can greatly improve the performance of some programs, they often make the programs more difficult to maintain. Because of this, the techniques must not be applied when they are not needed and appropriate. In Chapter 3 we will discuss when a programmer should worry about efficiency at all, and when tools other than writing efficient code are more appropriate for the job at hand.

The heart of this book is Chapters 4 and 5, which describe a set of rules for making programs more efficient. The rules of Chapter 4 deal with modifications to data structures and the rules of Chapter 5 deal with modifications to small pieces of program text. Each rule is given first as a brief statement, and is then illustrated by a small program that incorporates the rule, brief descriptions of how the rule has been used in large systems, or references to the literature where the reader may find further discussions of the rule.

The techniques described in Chapters 4 and 5 are applicable to most computer systems, and are almost independent of the system on which the final program is executed. There are, however, a set of techniques that will make programs run faster on some systems but might decrease performance on others. We will discuss the general topic of system-dependent efficiency in Chapter 6. That chapter starts with several examples, and then turns to a set of general principles. Because of the wide variation between systems, the principles take the form of questions a programmer should ask, and not the answers to those questions.

In Chapter 7 we will integrate the material of the previous chapters by studying it from the viewpoint of a programmer who would like to solve a particular problem. We will then illustrate the material in context in Chapter 8 as we study the two important programming problems of sorting and searching.

This book assumes that the reader has an extensive background in reading and writing code, and some experience with a high-level computer language. The tools that we will examine are like the surgeon's scalpel: they are very useful when applied in the right circumstances but disastrous if applied inappropriately. Their proper application must therefore be grounded in extensive programming experience. The programs in this book are written in Pascal; for the reader not familiar with that language, Appendix D includes a complete (small) Pascal program and a glossary of Pascal constructs used in this book. A background in algorithms and data structures, assembly language programming, and techniques for analyzing the correctness and efficiency of programs would be useful in reading parts of this book, but it is not necessary. In particular, the book never assumes background along these lines for more than a paragraph or two at a time, so the reader not versed in these areas will not miss much.

1.4 A SURVEY OF OTHER WORK

In this section we will briefly survey some previous work concerning writing efficient code. One line of research at this level goes under the name of "source-to-source program transformations". The goal of that research is to describe precisely a set of transformations at the source language level that preserve program correctness but increase program speed. The insistence on precise description of transformations has resulted in a set of transformations more accurately defined than those in Chapter 5, but unfortunately also less powerful. Examples of program transformations can be found in Burstall and Darlington [1977], Darlington and Burstall [1976], Loveman [1977], and Scherlis [1980]. Standish, Harriman, Kibler and Neighbors [1976] give a catalog of transformations that is an excellent reference and provides delightful browsing. Feign [1980] catalogs a number of transformations used to achieve very efficient assembly code. Nelson [1981] and Sproull [1981a] both use informal source-to-source transformations to write efficient code; Nelson uses many of the techniques in Chapters 4 and 5 to reduce the cost of a remote procedure call by a factor of over thirty.

Some programming texts include discussions of writing efficient code. For instance, Goodman and Hedetniemi [1977, Section 4.2] discuss this topic under the title of "implementation efficiency". They mention aspects of Loop Rules 1, 3 and 6, Logic Rule 3, and Expression Rules 2 and 3 (which we will study in Chapters 4 and 5). Kernighan and Plauger [1976, 1978] describe a number of issues related to writing efficient code; these are listed in their indices under the headings "algorithm", "efficiency", "optimization", "running time", and "time complexity", among others. Kreitzberg and Shneiderman [1972, Chapters 2 and 3] describe techniques for writing efficient FORTRAN code. Although many of their techniques are peculiar to that language (and some even to certain compilers), they include many general rules for reducing time and space costs.

Waldbaum [1978] describes the effect that writing efficient code can have on the throughput of a large (scientific) computer installation. In a six-month study at the IBM Yorktown Computer Center, Waldbaum's group reduced the time of twenty large programs by at least fifty percent, and in one case by ninety-five percent. This effort lead to a marked improvement in turnaround and response time for the system as a whole. Waldbaum describes many of the improved programs in detail, and discusses some of the general principles underlying the particular optimizations.

Jalics [1977] and Smith [1978] provide nice introductions to issues of efficiency in data processing systems. Jalics discusses a number of issues at various design levels including file organization and the efficiency of various language constructs. He mentions several of the rules that we will see in Chapters 4 and 5, including Space-For-Time Rule 3, Loop Rule 1, Logic Rule 3, and Procedure Rules 1 and 2. He also provides many concrete examples of increasing the efficiency of data processing systems. Smith covers in detail many of the important issues in system efficiency. She discusses the issues at various design levels including reducing costly input/output operations, reducing paging, and data structure selection, and compiler optimization. The techniques of writing efficient code that she discusses include Loop Rules 1, 2, 3 and 6, Procedure Rule 2, and Expression Rule 2. She addresses a number of important points in applying efficiency improvements, such as selecting the programs to modify and the management of efficiency improvements. She also presents details on the improvement of the efficiency of several systems.

Several authors have discussed writing efficient code for microcomputers and home computers. Lewis [1979] describes eight general rules for efficiency, and Noyce [1978] reduces the running time of a multiplication routine by 25% (and describes how it could be reduced by an additional 25%). Gunther [1981] describes several techniques for increasing the speed of BASIC programs.

There is a treasure-house of information about writing efficient code in the works of Donald Knuth. His textbooks (Knuth [1968, 1969, 1973]) are classics in the fields of algorithms and data structures, and are laden with both examples and principles of writing efficient code. His empirical study of FORTRAN programs (Knuth [1971]) gave a precise perspective to the activity of writing efficient code; we will see in Chapter 3 how his study allows us to ignore efficiency most of the time and concentrate on it when it really matters. That paper also contains seventeen detailed examples of efficient translations of FORTRAN fragments into IBM System/360 assembly code. Knuth [1974] is an excellent study of the question of how programming language design and programming methodologies relate to writing efficient code. In fact, of the twenty-seven efficiency rules in Chapters 4 and 5, fifteen refer explicitly to the works of Knuth. In addition to his own works, many of the Stanford Ph.D. theses and other papers of Professor Knuth's students are invaluable studies in writing efficient code; in later chapters we will see the works of Sedgewick [1975, 1978], Mont-Reynaud [1976], and Van Wyk [1981].

1.5 EXERCISES

1.1. The purpose of this exercise is to compare the costs of programmer time and computer time. We will assume that a programmer costs a company $50,000 per year (unfortunately, not all of that is salary) or $25.00 per hour, and that an hour of processor time costs the company $120.00. Finally, we will assume that an industrious programmer has just spent one hour making a change that decreases the run time of a certain program fragment by ten microseconds (and most changes to large software systems require much longer than an hour to incorporate). Under the following assumptions, how much money per day will the change save the company? How long will it take for the change to pay for itself? (That is, when will the value in dollars of the processor time saved equal the cost in programmer time of making the change?)

   a. The fragment is in the prologue of a program that is executed once per day.

   b. The fragment is executed 10,000 times in each execution of a program; the program is executed ten times per day.

   c. The fragment is executed 100,000 times in each execution of a program; the program is executed 100 times per day.

   d. The fragment is the procedure call mechanism in a high-level language, and is executed one billion times per day.

1.2. Discuss efficiency improvements possible at the design levels of Section 1.2 for systems that accomplish the following tasks. Concentrate your discussions on the levels of system structure (Exactly what problem will the system solve? How will the inputs be given? What is a good decomposition of the system into modules?), intramodular structure (What algorithms and data structures should be incorporated?), system software (What primitive operations should be built or modified?), and hardware (What special-purpose hardware should be considered?).

   a. **Compilation.** The system is to translate a high-level language (such as Pascal) into the machine language of a particular system.

   b. **Document Production.** The system is to translate a description of a document into a form suitable for printing. Reid's [1980] Scribe document production system (which was used to prepare this book) is particularly interesting to study.

2

AN EXAMPLE

This chapter introduces the activity of writing efficient code by studying one small program in detail.[1] The program deals with one particular problem, but our interest in the program has a much broader base than the problem it solves.

- The problem arose in a real system, and the program we will study was implemented in that system.
- The techniques of writing efficient code increase the speed of a Pascal program by a factor of almost seven; this reduced the program's time from half a CPU hour per day to less than five minutes per day.
- Similar techniques can be used in an assembly language implementation of the program to yield another speedup of a factor of ten; the overall program speedup is a factor of seventy.
- All of the improvements we will see are achieved by applying general techniques from Chapters 4 and 5.

The problem we will solve is defined in Section 2.1. We will increase the speed of a Pascal program to solve the problem in Section 2.2, and then briefly study an assembly code implementation of the resulting program in Section 2.3. Finally, the lessons of this chapter are summarized in Section 2.4.

---

[1]Readers interested in additional detailed studies of concrete examples should see Chapter 8 (especially Section 8.2).

2.1 PROBLEM DEFINITION

The object of our study in this chapter will be the planar *Traveling Salesman Problem*: the input is a set of N points in the plane (which we often think of as cities), and we must produce as output a minimal-length tour of the points. A tour of the cities is defined to be a list that contains each city exactly once; the length of the tour is the sum of the distance from the first city to the second plus the distance from the second to third and so on, finally ending with the distance from the Nth city back to the first. A set of points is shown in Figure 2.1a, and their traveling salesman tour is shown in Figure 2.1b. This problem arose in the context of scheduling a mechanical plotter to draw marks at about one thousand points: we would like to plot the marks in an order that does not waste much time moving from one point to the next.

The problem of efficiently finding a tour of a set of points with absolutely minimal total length has been studied for almost a century and is still unsolved; many people think that some day we will be able to prove that one cannot efficiently find an optimal tour. (See, for example, Lewis and Papadimitriou [1978].) We will therefore be concerned with quickly finding a relatively good, if not optimal, tour; this is ideal in the plotter application, and appropriate in many other applications. The following algorithm has been observed to give tours whose lengths are usually within about 25% of optimal.

> **The Nearest Neighbor Heuristic:** Choose an arbitrary starting point, and then repeatedly visit the unvisited point closest to the current point until all points have been visited. When this is accomplished, close the tour by returning to the starting point.

Figure 2.1c shows the Nearest Neighbor tour of the point set in Figure 2.1a; the starting point of the tour is circled. For details on the performance of this heuristic, see Bentley and Saxe [1980].

In this section we will study a Pascal procedure that implements the heuristic. The initial version of the procedure has a running time of approximately $47.0N^2$ microseconds on a Digital Equipment Corporation PDP-KL10; it therefore required about 47 seconds to construct the tour of a set of one thousand cities. That program was used in two distinct applications. In the first it was run several dozen times per day on a Digital Equipment Corporation PDP-KL10, and therefore consumed about half an hour of CPU time per day. In the other it was run only about a dozen times per day, but on a machine that was only about half as fast as a PDP-KL10; it also required about half an hour per day of CPU time. In both applications, that amount of time was excessive, so we are justified in expending energy in trying to do so.

The purpose of this exercise is to see how we can achieve efficiency by working only at the design level of writing efficient code. The first ground rule we must obey says that we cannot work at lower design levels.

Changes that we make must decrease the running time of the Pascal

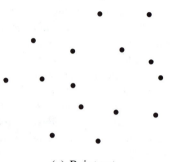

(a) Point set.

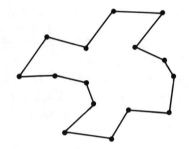

(b) An optimal tour.

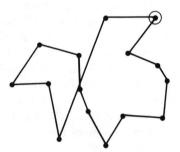

(c) A nearest-neighbor tour.

Figure 2.1. A point set and two tours.

program on most systems; we cannot make changes that exploit a particular feature of the compiler or hardware we happen to be using.

The next ground rule says that we cannot increase efficiency by working at the higher design level of changing algorithms and data structures.

The nearest neighbor program must operate by inspecting the distances to all unvisited cities as it looks for the next city on the tour.

As we study the Pascal program we will not examine the machine code that the compiler generates; our only view of the program's speed will be by using a built-in time function. The Hamburg Pascal compiler used for this experiment does little optimization, so the computation that we see in the source code accurately reflects the machine code from which times were collected. Details on the compiler and the timings can be found in Appendix A. To make sure that the timings are not merely artifacts of the particular compiler and hardware, the programs of this section were also implemented in a different language on a different computing system, and produced a similar set of relative timings (those timings can also be found in Appendix A).

We will now investigate a series of Pascal programs that implement the Nearest Neighbor Heuristic for the Traveling Salesman Problem. As we do so, the reader should attempt to improve each successive program before reading the next.

2.2 A SEQUENCE OF PASCAL CODE FRAGMENTS

The first subroutine for implementing the nearest neighbor heuristic for the traveling salesman problem is shown in Fragment A1. It assumes several external definitions: a variable of type PtPtr (for "point pointer") is an integer in the range 1..MaxPts, where MaxPts denotes the maximum possible number of points in the plane. The points themselves are stored in an array PtArr[PtPtr], whose elements are records with the two real components X and Y. The number of points in the array is stored in the integer variable NumPts; we will often refer to NumPts as N, since it is the problem size. The subroutine Dist is passed two PtPtr's, and returns the Euclidean distance between the two points (the code for the function will be shown in Fragment A3).

The operation of procedure ApproxTSTour is straightforward. The only data structure it uses besides the array PtArr is the array Visited[PtPtr] of boolean; the element Visited[I] is true if and only if point I has already been visited in the tour. The routine's first action is to initialize every element of that array to false and then to choose the first point to be visited as PtArr[NumPts] (the last point in the array). It then goes into a loop in which it selects the next NumPts − 1 points on the tour. To select each point it finds the closest point not yet visited, and then makes that point the current point. The `writeln` statements produce a description of the tour on the output file; they were not actually present in the version used for the timings and will not henceforth be shown in the program fragments. The program is simple; excluding lines that contain only `begin`, `end` or `writeln` statements, it contains only thirteen executable lines of code.

```pascal
procedure ApproxTSTour;
  var I, J: PtPtr;
    Visited: array [PtPtr] of boolean;
    ThisPt, ClosePt: PtPtr;
    CloseDist: real;

  begin
  (* Initialize unvisited points *)
  for I := 1 to NumPts do
    Visited[I] := false;

  (* Choose NumPts as starting point *)
  ThisPt := NumPts;
  Visited[NumPts] := true;
  writeln('First city is ', NumPts);

  (* Main loop of nearest neighbor heuristic *)
  for I := 2 to NumPts do
    begin
  (* Find nearest unvisited point to ThisPt *)
    CloseDist := maxreal;
    for J := 1 to NumPts do
      if not Visited[J] then
        if Dist(ThisPt, J) < CloseDist then
          begin
          CloseDist := Dist(ThisPt, J);
          ClosePt := J
          end;
    (* Report closest point *)
    writeln('Move from', ThisPt, 'to', ClosePt);
    Visited[ClosePt] := true;
    ThisPt := ClosePt
    end;

  (* Finish tour by returning to start *)
  writeln('Move from', ThisPt, 'to', NumPts)
  end;
```

Fragment A1. Original code.

The main for loop of the program is executed $N-1$ times, and contains an inner loop that is itself executed N times; the total time required by the program will therefore be dominated by a term proportional to N^2. The Pascal running time of Fragment A1 was observed to be approximately $47.0N^2$

microseconds (details on measurements of the running time can be found in Appendix A). **[Note to the brave reader: See Exercise 2.1 now.]**

We will now modify the program to increase its speed. As we do so, we should concentrate on the inner loop ("for J := 1 to NumPts do ... "), because each statement in that loop is executed $N^2 - N$ times, while every other statement is executed at most N times. A potential inefficiency in that loop is the fact that the real-valued result of Dist(ThisPt,J) can be calculated twice for each distinct value of J in the inner loop. We will instead calculate it just once, store it, and then use that stored value twice. Since this can decrease the number of distance calculations by a factor of two, we might expect it to cut the run time of the program almost in half. The modified code is shown in Fragment A2; it stores Dist(ThisPt,J) in the real variable ThisDist. All the lines that have been changed from Fragment A1 are marked with a vertical bar on the right.

```
begin
ThisDist := Dist(ThisPt, J);
if ThisDist < CloseDist then
   begin
   CloseDist := ThisDist;
   ClosePt := J
   end
end
```

Fragment A2.   Store ThisDist.

Only portions of the code changed from Fragment A1 are shown in Fragment A2; the remainder of Fragment A2 is from the corresponding parts of Fragment A1.

When I first made this change I was eagerly waiting to see a factor of almost two squeezed out of the run time, and I was shocked to see it drop from $47.0N^2$ microseconds to $45.6N^2$ microseconds! After observing these times, though, it was easy to explain what had happened. The then clause of the inner if statement is executed rarely, so in Fragment A1 the subroutine Dist was usually called only once per loop. Specifically, we can prove that the average number of times that the then branch is executed when there are M points left unvisited is

$$H_M = 1 + 1/2 + 1/3 + 1/4 + ... + 1/M,$$

which is called "the M-th harmonic number" and is approximately equal to the natural logarithm of M (H_{1000} is about 7.5). For a more detailed analysis of this fascinating combinatorial problem, see Section 1.2.10 of Knuth [1968]. Empirical observations that confirm this analysis can be found in Appendix A. This example illustrates a common experience in writing efficient code: changes that we expect to yield a big savings of time often make but a small difference.

Even though this improvement did not yield a great time reduction, it did isolate an important part of the problem: computing the distances between pairs of points.

Is there any way we can improve the procedure Dist for calculating distances shown at the top of Fragment A3? Unfortunately, it appears that we cannot; that procedure succinctly expresses the mathematical definition of Euclidean distances. We can, however, solve a different problem more efficiently: since all we ever do (in this procedure) is compare the relative magnitude of two distances, we do not need to take the square root of the sum of the squares before we return the result. That is, we can compare the squares of the distances to decide which point is closer; this relies on the monotonicity of the square root function (which says that for nonnegative x and y, x is greater than y if and only if $sqrt(x)$ is greater than $sqrt(y)$). The resulting code is shown at the bottom of Fragment A3.

```
function Dist(I,J: PtPtr): real;
  begin
  return sqrt(sqr(PtArr[I].X-PtArr[J].X) +
          sqr(PtArr[I].Y-PtArr[J].Y))
  end;

function DistSqrd(I,J: PtPtr): real;
  begin
  return sqr(PtArr[I].X-PtArr[J].X) +
        sqr(PtArr[I].Y-PtArr[J].Y)
  end;


. . .
ThisDist := DistSqrd(ThisPt, J);
. . .
```

Fragment A3.   Remove square roots.

This improvement does indeed lead to a substantial time savings: while Fragment A2 required $45.6N^2$ microseconds, Fragment A3 requires only $24.2N^2$ microseconds. This difference is almost a factor of two. Since removing $\binom{N}{2} = N(N-1)/2$ square roots saved $21.4N^2$ microseconds, we can deduce that each square root required about 43 microseconds.

There is still one glaring deficiency in the organization of the program. Suppose we are solving the problem for one thousand cities and we have only ten unvisited cities; how do we find the closest city to ThisPt? We look at all one thousand cities, only to find that most of them have already been visited. It would be more efficient for us to keep track of the unvisited cities in a way that would enable us to ignore the visited cities. This is accomplished in Fragment A4, which is a complete rewrite of Fragment A1, incorporating the changes of

Fragments A2 and A3. (This is the most substantial change we will make to the Pascal program, and indeed the most substantial *kind* of change that falls under the heading of writing efficient code; this change might be better classified as a selection of data structures, and therefore at a higher design level.) The initial portion of the array UnVis contains integer pointers (that is, PtPtr's) to un-visited elements of PtArr; specifically, the indices of all unvisited cities can always be found in UnVis[1..HighPt]. The overall structure of the routine is almost unchanged. The initialization is somewhat different, and the structure of the inner loop is different: the for statement runs from 1 to the current num-ber of points (HighPt), and no if test is required. When the closest point has been identified it is swapped with the point in UnVis[HighPt] and HighPt is decreased by one; this maintains the invariant condition that all unvisited cities can be found in UnVis[1..HighPt].[2]

[2]Some readers might wonder why we use an array of pointers rather than a linked list; exploring the latter approach shows that linked lists require approximately twice as much space, and are also slightly more expensive in time.

```pascal
procedure ApproxTSTour;
  var
    I: PtPtr;
    UnVis: array [PtPtr] of PtPtr;
    ThisPt, HighPt, ClosePt, J: PtPtr;
    CloseDist, ThisDist: real;
  procedure SwapUnVis(I, J: PtPtr);
    var Temp: PtPtr;
    begin
    Temp := UnVis[I];
    UnVis[I] := UnVis[J];
    UnVis[J] := Temp
    end;

  begin
  (* Initialize unvisited points *)
  for I := 1 to NumPts do
  UnVis[I] := I;
  (* Choose NumPts as starting point *)
  ThisPt := UnVis[NumPts];
  HighPt := NumPts-1;
  (* Main loop of nearest neighbor tour *)
  while HighPt > 0 do
    begin
    (* Find nearest unvisited point to ThisPt *)
    CloseDist := maxreal;
    for I := 1 to HighPt do
      begin
      ThisDist := DistSqrd(UnVis[I],ThisPt);
      if ThisDist < CloseDist then
        begin
        ClosePt := I;
        CloseDist := ThisDist
        end
      end;
    (* Report this point *)
    ThisPt := UnVis[ClosePt];
    SwapUnVis(ClosePt,HighPt);
    HighPt := HighPt-1
    end
  end;
```

Fragment A4.   Convert boolean array to pointer array.

The result of this change is to decrease the running time from $24.2N^2$ microseconds to $21.2N^2$ microseconds; it cut the loop overhead in half and eliminated testing, but introduced new indirect addressing through the array Un-Vis. In many systems this change will increase the program's space requirements; while each of the N elements of Visited requires just one bit, each of the N elements of UnVis requires one word. There is, however, an unexpected benefit of using this extra storage: upon completion of the routine, the Nearest Neighbor tour can be found in reverse order in the array UnVis. (We will return to this fact as we study Time-For-Space Rule 1 in Section 4.2.)

From this point on we will concentrate on the inner for loop, which is responsible for almost all of the run time. From our knowledge that the if test is rarely successful, we can deduce that most of the time is spent in the subroutine DistSqrd. To reduce its time, we will rewrite its body in line; this eliminates the overhead of the procedure calls. We then observe that some invariant expressions are reevaluated each time through the loop (namely, the array indexing of PtArr[ThisPt]), so we instead assign those outside the loop to the real variables ThisX and ThisY. The resulting code is shown in Fragment A5; its running time is $14.0N^2$ microseconds (a reduction of $7.2N^2$ from Fragment A4).

```
(* Find nearest unvisited to ThisPt *)
ThisX := PtArr[ThisPt].X;
ThisY := PtArr[ThisPt].Y;
CloseDist := maxreal;
for I := 1 to HighPt do
  begin
  ThisDist := sqr(PtArr[UnVis[I]].X-ThisX)
            + sqr(PtArr[UnVis[I]].Y-ThisY);
  if ThisDist < CloseDist then
    begin
    ClosePt := I;
    CloseDist := ThisDist
    end
  end;
```

Fragment A5.   Rewrite procedure in line and remove invariants.

We can now see precisely where the time of the program is spent. When M cities are unvisited, it calculates ThisDist M times, makes M comparisons with CloseDist, and then executes the then branch H_M times, on the average. Since the H_M term is too small to worry about (remember, it is 7.5 out of 1000) and all M comparisons seem necessary, we had better concentrate on calculating ThisDist. It contains two terms; is there some way we can reduce those to one? Such a reduction is shown in Fragment A6: we first compute the x-distance from the Ith point to ThisVert, and if that alone is greater than

CloseDist, then we need not examine the y-distance. (Because the second term is positive, it can only increase ThisDist.)

```
ThisDist := sqr(PtArr[UnVis[I]].X-ThisX);        |
if ThisDist < CloseDist then                     |
  begin                                          |
  ThisDist := ThisDist +                         |
                sqr(PtArr[UnVis[I]].Y-ThisY);    |
  if ThisDist < CloseDist then                   |
    begin
    ClosePt := I;
    CloseDist := ThisDist
    end
  end                                            |
```

Fragment A6.   Delay computing y-distance.

Fragment A6 will be faster than Fragment A5 if the x-distance alone is usually sufficient to discard the point from consideration. A heuristic analysis suggests and experimental evidence confirms the conjecture that the number of times the y-distance must be considered is only about $2.25M^{1/2}$, where M is the current number of points; thus for 1000 points, only about 70 need have their y-values examined. (Details on the number of y-values examined can be found in Appendix A.) Observations of the running time of Fragment A6 confirm the efficacy of the approach: it reduced the running time from the $14.0N^2$ microseconds of Fragment A5 to $8.2N^2$ microseconds.

Fragment A6 appears to be the best we can do with the current structure, and in many applications we should halt our quest for efficiency at this point. We are going to have to be really sneaky to squeeze out any more time. We know that most of the time is going to computing a difference and a product of real numbers; is there any way to reduce that?[3] We can now use the fact that integer arithmetic is faster than real arithmetic on many machines, and convert the arithmetic from real to integer. The reader should complain that the cost difference is there for a good reason: real arithmetic solves a different problem. Henceforth we can advertise this program as finding only an approximation to a Nearest Neighbor tour, but we should remember that we already accepted the fact that a nearest neighbor tour gives only an approximation to the true tour. Moreover, we can deduce from a larger context that this approximation will usually not be far from the length of the Nearest Neighbor tour (we will not go into the details here).

---

[3]One way to reduce the cost is to replace the multiplication by taking an absolute value (we then have the x-distance itself rather than its square) and compare that to the distance to ClosePt (not the square of that distance). On the particular system used for this test, the cost of computing an absolute value is as much as the cost of a square, so we did not follow this path. It would have been beneficial on machines without fast multipliers. We will return to this approach in Appendix B.

The specific mechanism of Fragment A7 is to copy the points in `PtArr` (which we will assume have each coordinate between 0 and 1) to the array In-tArr in which each coordinate is in the range 1..10000. We then perform all operations in this integer domain. Fragment A7 defines types `SmallInt` (for the "small integer" coordinates) and `BigInt` (for the sum of squares of differences of coordinates). The resulting program is shown in Fragment A7; its run time is $7.5N^2$ microseconds, for a reduction of $0.7N^2$ microseconds or about ten percent.

```
procedure ApproxTSTour;
  type
    SmallInt = 0..10000;
    BigInt = 0..10000000000;
    IntPoint = record
      X, Y: SmallInt
      end;
  var
    I: PtPtr;
    UnVis: array [PtPtr] of PtPtr;
    ThisPt, HighPt, ClosePt, J: PtPtr;
    CloseDist, ThisDist: BigInt;
    ThisX, ThisY: SmallInt;
    IntArr: array [PtPtr] of IntPoint;

  procedure SwapUnVis(I, J: PtPtr);
    *** Unchanged

  begin
  (* Build IntArr *)
  for I := 1 to NumPts do
    begin
    IntArr[I].X := round(PtArr[I].X * 10000);
    IntArr[I].Y := round(PtArr[I].Y * 10000)
    end;
```

*** **The remainder of the code is changed as follows.**
*** **The built-in function "maxreal" is replaced by "10000000000".**
*** **References to PtArr are replaced by IntArr.**
```
  end;
```

Fragment A7.   Convert reals to integers.

Because real arithmetic is faster than integer arithmetic on some systems, the above change could actually decrease the program's performance on some architectures, while on other machines (especially minis and micros) it could lead to a savings of one or two orders of magnitude. Regardless of that possible savings, though, Fragment A7 points out another opportunity for time savings: we can now remove the level of indirection imposed by the UnVis array. Since we copied our new version of the points into IntArr, we can now permute those to keep all the unvisited cities in IntArr[1..HighPt], and do away entirely with the array UnVis. (We did not before have the freedom to alter the values in PtArr—other routines might depend on those values being in a particular order.) The resulting code is shown in Fragment A8; its running time is $6.9N^2$ microseconds, which is another improvement of about ten percent. (Fragment A8 also assumes that procedure SwapUnVis has been modified to swap values in IntArr.)

```
(* Find nearest unvisited to ThisPt *)
ThisX := IntArr[ThisPt].X;
ThisY := IntArr[ThisPt].Y;
CloseDist := 10000000000;
for I := 1 to HighPt do
  begin
  ThisDist := sqr(IntArr[I].X-ThisX);
  if ThisDist < CloseDist then
    begin
    ThisDist := ThisDist +
                sqr(IntArr[I].Y-ThisY);
    if ThisDist < CloseDist then
      begin
      ClosePt := I;
      CloseDist := ThisDist
      end
    end
  end;
```

Fragment A8.   Remove UnVisited array.

We now have a fast program. All that usually happens in each iteration of the inner loop is an array access, a subtraction, a multiplication, and a comparison, all of which seem necessary. The only overhead that does not perform a useful service is that of the for statement itself, which we will now try to eliminate. There are two aspects of the for statement: it increments I and tests to see whether I equals the termination value. Since it seems hard to avoid the cost of incrementing I (although we will see later that it can be done), we will try to make the second aspect faster by finding a better way to test for termination of the loop. The approach taken in Fragment A9 exploits the fact that ThisPt is stored in position HighPt + 1. Because the distance from ThisPt to itself is always zero, it would always be assigned as its own closest point, so we can put the test for loop termination into that part of the code that is executed only H_M times on the average, when M points are left. The one other change in the program is that we must ensure that points of distance zero from ThisPt are indeed assigned as ClosePt; that involves changing a ">=" to a ">" in the fifth and ninth lines of Fragment A9. The time of Fragment A9 is $6.8N^2$ microseconds, a savings of $0.1N^2$ microseconds over the time of Fragment A8, or less than a two percent reduction.

```
    I := 0;
Start:
    I := I+1;
    ThisDist := sqr(IntArr[I].X-ThisX);
    if ThisDist > CloseDist then
      goto Start;
    ThisDist := ThisDist +
    sqr(IntArr[I].Y-ThisY);
    if ThisDist > CloseDist then
      goto Start;
    if I >= HighPt then goto Finish;
    ClosePt := I;
    CloseDist := ThisDist;
    goto Start;
Finish:
```

Fragment A9.   Put loop control inside inner test.

There are two important facts to note about Fragment A9. The first is that the program does specify less computation than Fragment A8—it does less loop control. The second fact is that many compilers would produce substantially faster code from Fragment A8 than from Fragment A9—they contain special knowledge about for loops and compile them quite efficiently.

2.3 AN ASSEMBLY PROGRAM

Because the nearest neighbor heuristic was in the time bottleneck of a system, it was worthwhile to improve the run time of the program implementing the heuristic; we have concentrated so far in this chapter on doing so by reorganizing the computation in the Pascal language. This is often good enough, but in certain applications we need a program that is faster yet. In those cases, we can work at a lower design level and recode the algorithm in assembly code to employ the full potential of the underlying machine architecture. Fragment A10 shows how the code of Fragment A9 can be translated into (a slightly augmented version of) IBM System/360-370 assembler language.

```
Registers: CloseDist, ThisDist, I, ThisX, YDist

        L    ThisX,MemThisX
        L    CloseDist,PosInf
        LA   I,Array-8
Start   LA   I,8(I)              increment I by one rec
        L    ThisDist,0(I)       ThisDist  :=
        SR   ThisDist,ThisX        (X[I]-ThisX)²
        MR   ThisDist,ThisDist     *
        CR   ThisDist,CloseDist  if ThisDist>CloseDist
        BH   Start                 then goto Start
        L    YDist,MemThisY      YDist:=(Y[I]-ThisY)²
        S    YDist,4(I)            *
        MR   YDist,YDist           *
        AR   ThisDist,YDist      add YDist to ThisDist
        CR   ThisDist,CloseDist  if ThisDist>CloseDist
        BH   Start                 then goto Start
        C    I,EndPtAdd          if I>=EndPtAdd
        BNL  Finish                then goto Finish
        ST   I,ClosePtAdd        ClosePt:=I
        LR   CloseDist,ThisDist  CloseDist:=ThisDist
        B    Start               goto Start
Finish EQU   *
```

Fragment A10.   Translate to assembly code.

This program is almost an exact translation of the inner loop of Fragment A9. It assumes that the array of points is stored as N consecutive (x,y) pairs of fullwords (that is, 32-bit words aligned on four-byte boundaries). The variables ThisX and ThisY from Fragment A9 are assumed to be stored in memory locations MemThisX and MemThisY. All the arithmetic in the program is carried out as 32-bit integers, but that could easily be changed to real numbers.

The primary activity of the main loop of the program is in the six lines of code starting at the line labeled Start. At that line the register variable I is incremented by eight bytes to point to the next point to be tested. The x-value of that point is loaded into the register variable ThisDist in the next line of code, and the two lines after that subtract ThisX from the x-value and square the difference. The fifth line then compares the squared difference to CloseDist, and the sixth line does a conditional branch that is almost always taken (that is, all but about $2.25M^{1/2}$ times when M points are left, from our discussion of Fragment A6).

A simple experiment was conducted to compare the speed of the assembly code of Fragment A10 with the speed of the code a typical Pascal compiler produces. Fragments A1 and A9 were compiled on an IBM

System/370 under the Pascal/VS compiler[4], and the compiled code and the code of Fragment A10 were assigned time costs according to the model described by Knuth [1971] (which is described in Appendix B). The Pascal compiler used in this experiment performed roughly the same level of optimization as the PDP-10 Pascal compiler used in the previous experiments. Fragment A10 had a dominant term of $6.5N^2$ time units, while the code compiled from Fragment A1 had a dominant term of $110.833N^2$ units[5] and the code compiled from Fragment A9 had a dominant term of $12.5N^2$ units. Fragment A9 is therefore approximately 8.9 times faster than Fragment A1 on this system, while Fragment A10 is over 17 times faster than the code compiled from Fragment A1.

The point of this section is that after using the techniques of writing system-independent efficient code (which gave a speedup of a factor of approximately seven on a PDP-KL10 and of approximately nine on an IBM System/360), careful hand-translation into assembly code can make the resulting program even faster (by a factor of about two). If we are willing to exploit the full potential of the underlying architecture by careful assembly-language coding (and recall that this topic is explicitly beyond the scope of this chapter), then we can achieve even greater speedups. In Appendix B we pursue exactly this course by employing the techniques of this book at the assembly code level; by so doing we achieve an assembly program that is approximately seventy times faster than the code compiled from Fragment A1.

2.4 WHAT HAVE WE LEARNED?

We have devoted a great deal of effort in this chapter to a small piece of code. Before studying the general principles underlying this example, we should pause for a moment to review what we have learned in the exercise.

The first thing that we saw was that this fragment was located in the bottleneck of a system and that it was indeed worthwhile to improve its running time. The techniques we have seen should be applied only to a bottleneck in an inefficient system.

We then studied the computation as embodied in a series of Pascal procedures. We started with a simple and correct program and performed a sequence of *transformations* that

---

[4]That compiler is IBM Program Number 5796-PNQ (an Installed User Program) and is described in the "Pascal/VS Programmer's Guide" (IBM Publication Number SH20-6162-0). The programs were compiled under Pascal/VS Release 1.0 on an IBM System/370 at the University of Texas at Austin.

[5]The dominant term of $110.833N^2$ time units can be apportioned among the various activities in the innermost loop of Fragment A1 as follows. Loop cost of "for J := 1 to NumPts": $10N^2$; testing "if not Visited[J]": $6.5N^2$; cost of square root in procedure Dist: $42.5N^2$; other costs of procedure Dist: $42.833N^2$; comparing result of Dist to CloseDist: $9.0N^2$.

- preserve the correctness of the program,
- usually increase the length and decrease the readability of the program text, and
- decrease the run time of the program.

The transformations and the transformed programs are summarized in Table 2.1.   One can easily see that the most important improvements in the program were A2 ◊ A3 (removing square roots) and A4 ◊ A6 (computing distances in line with delayed calculation of *y*-distance).   The transformations leading from Fragment A6 to Fragment A9 were not as clean as the previous transformations, and had less impact on the Pascal running time (the time of Fragment A9 is about twenty percent less than the time of Fragment A6).

Table 2.1. Summary of program improvements.

Fragment Modification	Time/N^2	Time Change
A1.	47.0	
Store ThisDist		1.4
A2.	45.6	
Remove square roots		21.4
A3.	24.2	
Convert boolean array to pointer array		3.0
A4.	21.2	
Rewrite procedure in line and remove invariant expressions		7.2
A5.	14.0	
Delay computing y-distance		5.8
A6.	8.2	
Convert reals to integers		0.7
A7.	7.5	
Remove unvisited array		0.6
A8.	6.9	
Put loop control inside inner test		0.1
A9.	6.8	

Although the final three transformations did not greatly decrease the Pascal running time, they did pave the way for an elegant and efficient assembly program.   Transform A6 ◊ A7 (converting reals to integers) increased the storage of the program and made only a slight difference in time; it was included primarily to avoid the intricacies of real arithmetic in the assembly code.   It did point the way to Transform A7 ◊ A8 (removing the array UnVis), which reduced the overhead in the resulting assembly code.   Transform A8 ◊ A9 (loop control inside the inner test) led to an efficient inner loop in the assembly code. The part of the inner loop that is usually executed contains only six lines of assembly code.   Calculations showed that for large values of *N*, the assembly code of Fragment A10 is over seventeen times faster than the code a typical compiler produced from the Pascal Fragment A1. This efficient program was easy to code from Fragment A9; it would be difficult to achieve an assembly program of comparable efficiency by coding directly from Fragment A1.

The relative timings of the above fragments under the Hamburg Pascal compiler on the PDP-KL10 are typical of their timings under a broad class of compilers and computers (timings under another compiler and computer can be found in Appendix A). The relative timings might be different, though, under an optimizing compiler that automatically performs some of the transformations. Most compilers that I know do not perform any of the transformations. The only transformations even remotely within reach of highly optimizing compilers are A1 ◊ A2 (Store ThisDist—but this would require extensive interprocedural data flow analysis) and A4 ◊ A5 (Rewrite a procedure in line and remove invariant expressions). Each of the eight of transformations of this section should therefore lead to increased performance under most compilers.

We should keep in mind the purpose of studying the assembly code. It was not to illustrate any sophisticated assembly coding techniques; Fragment A10 is a straightforward translation of Fragment A9. Rather, the experience showed how good system-independent coding leads to good system-dependent code: even if our original goal had been to implement the assembly program, we would have been wise to perform the high-level changes before considering low-level issues.

The above discussion has been in an abstract context; we will now consider the problem in the two concrete applications mentioned at the start of this section. In the first application I had to write a Pascal program that was executed on thousand-city problems several dozen times per day over a period of a few weeks; I used the program of Fragment A6 (the nature of some of the inputs made difficult the conversion from reals to integers). The changes reduced the run time from approximately half an hour per day to less than five minutes per day. In the second application the programmer in charge had to develop a FORTRAN program that would be executed on thousand-city problems around a dozen times per day over approximately a one-year period. The basic structure was that of Fragment A6; again, the reals were not converted to integers. In both applications the original clean code was left in the program (as comments), along with documentation showing how the dirty program was derived from the clean program.

The optimizations we have seen so far in this chapter have ignored speedups possible by changing algorithms and data structures; such improvements are examined in Exercise 2.2. Changes at that level were not incorporated in the above programs because they required too much code for an insignificant improvement in performance (in both applications, half an hour per day was far too much run time, while five minutes was quite reasonable).

To summarize this chapter, our work on the Nearest Neighbor Heuristic has shown us the following:

- An increase of a factor of almost seven in the speed of a particular Pascal program.

- An efficient assembly program (translated from the Pascal program) that is seventeen times faster than the object code produced by a typical compiler.
- A methodology for increasing a program's speed while preserving its correctness: transformations at the source program level.

2.5 EXERCISES

2.1. This exercise is for the stout-hearted reader who would prefer to try his own hand at the program in this chapter before reading the development in the text. This exercise should be attempted after reading the text of Section 2.2 through the description of Fragment A1 (on page 16).

  a. [For assembly language programmers only.] Translate the Pascal program of Fragment A1 into the best assembly code you can. As long as you stick to the basic algorithm of finding the next city to visit by investigating all unvisited cities, you may make any change you want to the organization of the program. This chapter describes an efficient program in the IBM System/360-370 assembly code, but you may use whatever assembly language you wish.

  b. Increase the speed of Fragment A1 as much as you can in Pascal (or in the high-level language of your choice). Following the ground rules, you should make changes that decrease the running time of the program on most systems, and you should not try to exploit particular features of your compiler.

  c. [For assembly language programmers only.] After you have completed part b, go back and try part a again, but this time use any insights you gained in part b. Did these result in faster assembly code?

2.2. In this chapter we have increased the speed of the program for computing nearest neighbor tours by working at only two of the design levels mentioned in Section 1.2: writing efficient code and translation to assembly code. Both of these levels gave us an increase in the speed of the program of a factor of approximately seven; the total speedup on the two levels was a factor of approximately seventy (including the work described in Appendix B). The purpose of this exercise is to see what benefit we can achieve at the design level of the intramodular structure.

  a. Design efficient algorithms and data structures for implementing the nearest neighbor heuristic. You may assume that the points are approximately uniformly distributed over a square region of the plane. [Hint: group the points together spatially to avoid looking at all unvisited cities when you try to find the next city to visit. Relevant methods of grouping objects include sorting the points by one axis, dividing the square region into strips, and dividing the square region into cells. Bentley and Friedman [1979] discuss several of these approaches.] You should try to analyze the performance of your algorithm by telling how many distances it computes to find the nearest neighbor tour of N points.

  b. Implement your algorithm as a Pascal program (or in the high-level language of your choice). Make your code as clean as possible; in particular, don't trade clarity for efficiency. How does the run time of your program compare with the performance of Fragment A1 on your system? If your program is faster for large values of N, at what value of N is the break-even point? Compare your program in the same way to Fragment A9.

c. Now, apply the techniques of writing efficient code to your program and perform the two comparisons again (to Fragments A1 and A9). How many of the techniques used in this chapter were you able to apply to your program?

d. [For assembly language programmers only.] Code the program from part c into assembly language as efficiently as possible.

Reddy and Newell [1977] defend the hypothesis that in some systems speedups achieved at various design levels are independent and therefore multiply. In this exercise you have worked at three design levels: intramodular structure, writing efficient code, and translation to assembly code. What does your experience say about Reddy and Newell's hypothesis?

2.3. Implement the program in Fragment A1 as efficiently as possible (under the two ground rules of this chapter) on a different computing system. How many of the modifications of this chapter did you use, and how many were not appropriate?

2.4. In transforming Fragment A3 to A4 and Fragment A6 to A7 we decreased run time by adding space proportional to N. Suppose now that space is precious, and try to minimize the time taken by Fragment A1 without using much more than N extra bits of storage (which is the storage taken by the array Visited).

3

THE CONTEXT

The efficiency of a program is secondary when compared to the program's correctness: it is nice if a program is fast, but it is essential that it does what it claims to do. For this reason, efficiency should usually be a minor concern during the development of a program.[1] Kernighan and Plauger [1978, Chapter 7] present a number of programs that underscore the point that "premature optimization is the root of all evil", and Weinberg [1971, pp. 128-130] describes studies that show that striving for efficiency increases the time required to develop a program. The primary concerns of the programmer during the early part of a program's life should be the overall organization of the programming project (facing the issues described by Brooks [1975]) and producing correct and maintainable code (using the techniques of Kernighan and Plauger [1978], for instance). Furthermore, in many contexts, the cleanly designed program is often efficient enough for the application at hand.

Suppose, though, that you proceed as above and rapidly produce a correct, reliable and maintainable program that consumes enormous amounts of resources—what do you do then? The obvious next step is to modify the parts of the program you suspect are consuming the resources. There are two fundamental problems with this approach.

---

[1]As notable exceptions to this rule, Smith [1980, 1981] describes a methodology for estimating the performance of a large software system early in the development process, and Peterson [1980] applies algorithms and data structures early in the design of a module that he knows will be a bottleneck in the system.

1. Programmers are usually notoriously bad at guessing which parts of the code are the primary consumers of the resources. It is all too common for a programmer to modify a piece of code expecting to see a huge time savings and then to find that it makes no difference at all because the code was rarely executed. (We will see a vivid example of this in Section 3.3.)

2. The modifications made at the design level at which the programmer happens to be working might be less effective than modifications at other design levels. For instance, it is often most cost effective to change the intramodular structure (that is, the data structure and algorithms used in the module); sometimes, though, it is more effective to ignore other levels and use the techniques of writing efficient code to squeeze constant factors.

In Section 3.1 we will address the first problem by studying ways by which a programmer can locate the parts of a system that are consuming the most resources. Section 3.2 then studies the tools that programmers should bring to bear on those critical sections. These two aspects of "when to worry" and "what to do" are brought together in Section 3.3 as a methodology for building efficient computing systems.

3.1 WHEN TO WORRY

When a programmer finds that a certain program is too time-consuming, his first response should be to instrument the program to gather data on the time used by each part of the program (the parts might be either modules or procedures within modules). These statistics will identify the parts of the program that are using the most time, and the programmer can then focus his attention on those parts. The spectrum of methods for gathering statistics includes the following:

- In the best of all worlds, the programming language we use automatically provides us with a *profile* of our program that tells us how often each statement is executed and the amount of time spent in each procedure. Glancing at these statistics lets us see immediately what portions of code are executed most often. Additionally, our attention is quickly drawn to pieces of code that are never executed (Is our logic correct? Do we really need that code?), and to relations between various counts. Satterthwaite [1972] describes how such features were implemented in the Stanford University AlgolW compiler, and Bergeron and Bulterman [1975] describe a language-independent profiling facility for the IBM System/370. Knuth [1974] found these features so useful that he argued they should be supplied in all future compilers, and Sites [1978] gives arguments supporting the same point. Because instructions have different speeds, counts alone do not necessarily reflect the time taken by a particular piece of code; profiles should therefore provide times as well as counts.

- Even if profiles are not built into the system, it is usually not much more than a couple weeks' work to build a program that augments a high-level language program with the bookkeeping statements necessary to gather its own profile. The augmented program then writes these counts to a file at the end of execution, and a postprocessing program later reads that file and prepares a nicely formatted profile. This tool takes but a short while to build and can pay for itself quickly. Brailsford, Foxley, Mander, and Morgan [1977] describe such a system for the Algol 68 language, Matwin and Missala [1976] describe a machine-independent profiling system for Pascal, and Kernighan and Plauger [1976, Exercise 9-22] give some general hints for building such tools.

- As a simple last resort, it is usually easy to augment a program with timing statements that access a global system clock. To measure a routine's time we store the current time, call the routine, and when control is returned subtract the stored time from the current time, giving the time spent in the routine. This technique is described in detail by Wulf, Shaw, Hilfinger, and Flon [1981, Chapter 6]. There are several difficulties with this approach. First, we only learn the time of the routine we monitored, and programmers rarely monitor the right routine (remember, they are notoriously bad guessers). Second, unless the clock is quite accurate and the routine is relatively long, it is hard to measure the true time of the routine. (So if a routine takes only a hundred microseconds, we may never have our attention drawn to it.) Even with these disadvantages, this approach can still provide useful information; Appendix A describes how this technique was used to gather run times on the Pascal fragments of Chapter 2.

Plattner and Nievergelt [1981] survey the general problem of monitoring program execution (that is, the problem of observing the empirical behavior of programs), and the particular problem of observing program performance.

After solving the problem of *how* to monitor, we must still face the problem of *what* to monitor: on what input data shall we run our program to gather measurements? This question is easily answered for programs with control flow that is not strongly dependent on the input data: almost any input will do. For most systems, though, the programmer should monitor the program on input data that is typical of the data the program will encounter in production. Note that usual test data often does not meet this requirement: while test data is chosen to exercise all parts of the code, profiling data should be chosen for its "typicality".

Although the statistics on program times can be difficult to get, they almost always bring good news: a small part of the program text usually accounts for a high percentage of the run time. By decreasing the run time of that small part of the program, we dramatically improve the overall performance of the entire program. An early study along these lines was done by Knuth [1971]; he reported that for a set of twenty-four FORTRAN programs "less than four percent of a program generally accounts for more than half of its running time". Similar experiments have been repeated for large numbers of programs in many different languages, and similar results have usually been achieved. If we take Knuth's percentages as typical, then there are two important implications for programmers.

- If we speed up the four percent of the code that contains the inner loops, then we will speed up the entire program tremendously. For instance, if we increase their speed to require only half as much time as before, then the whole program will require only seventy-five percent as much time.

- Any efficiency improvement in the 96% of the code that isn't in the inner loops won't make much difference in the overall performance of the program.

As examples of this phenomenon, Fitch [1977] describes how small changes in an algebra system led to a seventy percent savings in run time, and Sites [1978] tells how local changes were used to reduce the run time of a Pascal compiler by about half. Waldbaum [1978] observed that this phenomenon is also exhibited in computer centers; in his study of five machines at the IBM Yorktown Computing Center, between one and five percent of the users accounted for over fifty per-cent of the run time on each machine. (His study also observed this phenomenon in individual programs.)

When we read program profiles we should concentrate our attention not only on the time-consuming procedures but also on how they are used. Suppose, for example, that we profiled a symbol table package and found that ninety per-cent of the time was spent in a routine that compares two strings. A naive ap-proach would speed up that operation, which might increase the overall speed of the program by (say) a factor of two. A more sophisticated approach would study how the string compare routine is used. This might show, for instance, that it was called so frequently because the symbol table's search routine was organized as a linear search. In that case, changing the search structure to hash-ing could easily increase the program's efficiency by a factor of ten.

3.2 WHAT TO DO

Once we identify the expensive parts of a system we should apply the ap-propriate efficiency tools; to do so we must keep in mind the design levels described in Section 1.2. Every computing system has been designed at all of the levels described there: the overall system structure, intramodular structure, efficient code, translation to machine code, underlying system software, and un-derlying hardware. If a system is inefficient, then we should try to gain ef-ficiency at the proper level. Sometimes that level is the overall system design: we should build a new system based on a new design (Brooks [1975, Chapter 11] advises us to "plan to throw one away; you will, anyhow"). In other systems we should rewrite the system software[2] or acquire new hardware. Most programmers, however, cannot take such extreme measures, so they must squeeze what efficiency they can from the middle band of levels: intramodular structure, writing efficient code, and translation to machine code. In this section we will concentrate on how a programmer should operate at those levels.

The programmer's primary weapon in the never-ending battle against slow systems is to change the intramodular structure. Our first response should be to reorganize the module's *data structures*. Brooks [1975, Chapter 9] accurately describes the importance of data structures: "representation is the essence of programming". By changing the representation of data, we can often drastically reduce the time required to operate on it. Courses in data structures are now well established in computer science curricula. Because of the central role played by data structures, expert programmers should be intimately familiar with the material in data structures texts such as Standish [1980]. Knuth [1968, 1973] is an excellent source for all aspects of data structure selection and implementation. We will return to the issue of data structures in Chapters 4 and 8.

The second tool we should consider at this point is the field of *algorithm design*. By changing the underlying technique used to solve a problem, one can often achieve tremendous savings in time. For instance, changing a sequential search subroutine to binary search will reduce the average number of comparisons required to search a sorted N-element table from about $N/2$ to just $\log_2 N$: for $N = 1000$, this is a reduction from 500 to 10. (We will see in Chapter 8, though, that the increased overhead of sophisticated algorithms can result in much larger constant factors than those of their simpler cousins; one must therefore be careful to determine the break-even point of two programs.) Proper algorithm design can lead to similar savings for many problems. Algorithm design and analysis is the subject of several texts, including Knuth [1968, 1969, 1973], Aho, Hopcroft, and Ullman [1974], Goodman and Hedetniemi [1977], Reingold, Nievergelt and Deo [1977], Baase [1978], and Horowitz and Sahni [1978]. For survey articles on the subject, see Lewis and Papadimitriou [1978] and Bentley [1979].

Once we have achieved all the possible efficiency at the intramodular level, we should attempt to speed up our system by writing efficient code. We must keep a perspective on the speedups achievable at this level: we can often increase the speed of a routine by a constant factor (say, from two to ten), but

---

[2]When Doug McIlroy [1981] monitored a time-consuming program that implemented a relational database operation he found that almost all of the time was spent in an input/output subroutine to back up a file (essentially, to "unread" the current record). Inspection of the code showed that the subroutine implemented the operation by re-reading the block of the previous record from disk, even though that block might have already been in main memory. Changing the subroutine to check for that case (and then avoiding the disk read) required only four lines of code and increased the speed of the particular program by a factor of over three; it also increased the speed of all other programs that made extensive use of backing up records.

we rarely achieve the dramatic kind of speedup that we experience in changing from a sequential search to a binary search. This activity will usually make our programs slightly more difficult to maintain (the code is more complicated), but it often substantially increases the efficiency of the system.

If the resulting program is still not efficient enough, then we can often increase its speed by recoding the crucial parts into assembly language. With certain optimizing compilers, it is not uncommon to find that the compiler produces code that is better than the code we produce by hand. On the other hand, it is often possible to produce code by hand that is much faster than the code of typical compilers (Appendix B shows how hand-coding gives us *another* factor of seven for the program in Chapter 2). Feign [1980] argues that assembly-language coding will play a crucial role in efficient systems for the foreseeable future, and catalogs many techniques assembly coders use to achieve efficiency.

3.3 A METHODOLOGY

To summarize the two previous sections, the following steps are essential parts of a methodology of building efficient computing systems.

1. The most important properties of a large system are a clean design and implementation, useful documentation, and maintainable modularity. The first steps in the programming process should therefore be the design of a solid system and the clean implementation of that design.

2. If the overall system performance is not satisfactory, then the programmer should monitor the program to identify where the scarce resources are being consumed. This usually reveals that most of the time is used by a few percent of the code.

3. Proper data structure selection and algorithm design are often the key to large reductions in the running time of the expensive parts of the program. The programmer should therefore try to revise the data structures and algorithms in the critical modules of the system.

4. If the performance of the critical parts is still unsatisfactory, then use the techniques of Chapters 4 and 5 to recode them. The original code should usually be left in the program as documentation.

5. If additional speed is still needed, then the programmer should work at lower design levels, including hand-written assembly code, operating system modifications, microcode, and special-purpose hardware design.

To make the above methodology more concrete, I would like to relate two war stories from Bell Telephone Laboratories. I had a discussion with Chris Van Wyk [1981] about the material of this section in the early afternoon on a Thursday; at 5:00 PM of that day he mentioned that he had successfully tried these techniques on one of his programs, and the next Monday I received from him the following mail.

My interpreter for IDEAL seemed to be awfully slow and to take a lot of space, so I profiled its execution. It turned out that over a sample of ten test cases that exercise every part of the code, it was spending almost seventy percent of its time in the system's memory allocator!

Further investigation revealed that most of this was used in allocating one particular kind of node (more than 68,000 times, with the next most popular node being allocated around 2,000 times). I added the minimal bookkeeping necessary to keep my own queue of free nodes of this particular kind, and reduced the memory allocator's share of the time to about thirty percent.

There were three benefits of this change:

1. less time in the allocator (it's a circular list with a roving pointer),
2. less memory fragmentation (our allocator doesn't compact), and
3. now that the statistics aren't overwhelmed by the allocator's share, I can find places that need to be sped up with sophisticated algorithms or data structures.

On the other hand, it would not be worth my time to provide my own bookkeeping for every kind of node I allocate, so I save programming effort on another front.

To make a long story short, by spending a few hours monitoring his program and then making a small change, Van Wyk was able to reduce the program's run time to about forty-five percent of what it was previously. (We will see in the next chapters that Van Wyk's modification can be viewed as an instance of Space-For-Time Rule 3 and Procedure Rule 2.) Notice that Van Wyk used two kinds of monitoring in this example: he first used the system profiler to determine that the storage allocator consumed most of the time, and then added bookkeeping code to the allocator to determine what kinds of nodes were most frequently allocated.

This discussion would not be complete without a story of *not* monitoring a program. Victor Vyssotsky [1981] enhanced a FORTRAN compiler in the early 1960's under the design constraint that compilation time could not be noticeably slower. A particular routine in his program was executed rarely (he estimated during design that it would be called in about one percent of the compilations, and just once in each of those) but was very slow, so Vyssotsky spent a week squeezing every last unneeded cycle out of the routine. The modified compiler was fast enough. After two years of extensive use the compiler reported an internal error during compilation of a program. When Vyssotsky inspected the code he found that the error occurred in the prologue of the "critical" routine, and that the routine had contained this bug for its entire production life. This implied that the routine had never been called during more than 100,000 compilations, so the week that Vyssotsky put into prematurely optimizing it was completely wasted.

3.4 EXERCISES

3.1. Choose a large program (preferably at least 500 lines of code) and determine its expensive parts in the following ways, in the order that they are described:

    a. From your knowledge of the program's use and inspection of the code, estimate the three most expensive procedures in the program. Guess what percentage of the total time is accounted for by each of the procedures.

    b. Use the system clock to measure the overall run time of the program and the time spent in each of the procedures you identified in part a.

    c. Use a program profiler to give the time spent in each procedure.

Were there any surprises in this exercise? Did it increase or decrease your confidence in your powers of estimation?

3.2. The purpose of this exercise is to compare the kinds of improvements achievable by writing efficient code and by changing algorithms. Suppose that a "slow" quadratic algorithm can be implemented easily as Program S1 with running time of $10N^2$ microseconds, and that we can improve that to yield Program S2 with running time of N^2 microseconds. Suppose also that a simple implementation of a "fast" algorithm results in Program F1 with time of $100N \log_2 N$ microseconds, which can then be reduced to $10N \log_2 N$ microseconds as Program F2. Make a table of the time required by the four programs for every power of ten between ten and one million. (Recall that $\log_2 10$ is approximately 3.32.)

4

MODIFYING DATA STRUCTURES

In this chapter we will study techniques that increase the efficiency of a program by making small modifications to the program's data structures. The best changes to make to a data structure from the viewpoint of efficiency are, of course, those that reduce both the program's time and space. A host of data structure texts (see, for example, Knuth [1968, 1973] and Standish [1980]) describe many sophisticated structures that can replace their simpler cousins and thereby reduce both the time and space requirements of a program. Throughout the remainder of this section, though, we will take a microscopic view of data structures, and try to find the best way to implement a particular structure once it has been chosen to represent the data. At this low level there are few changes that reduce both program time and space; most changes trade one resource for the other. In Section 4.1 we will study techniques that reduce a program's run time by increasing its space, and then study tradeoffs in the opposite direction in Section 4.2.

4.1 TRADING SPACE FOR TIME

We will start our study by investigating four techniques that increase space to decrease run time. Each one trades space for time by storing redundant information. The first such rule is the following:

> **Space-For-Time Rule 1—Data Structure Augmentation:** The time required for common operations on data can often be reduced by augmenting the structure with extra information or by changing the information within the structure so that it can be accessed more easily.

The example of Section 2.2 provides two instances of augmentation. In changing Fragment A3 to A4 we reduced the time spent in scanning bits by increasing the storage required to one pointer per word (rather than one bit). In removing the indirect addressing of Fragment A7 we duplicated an array in Fragment A8. *Reference counters* augment nodes in dynamically allocated storage with information that facilitates garbage collection of useless nodes; Knuth [1968, pp. 412-413] and Standish [1980, Section 5.4.3.1] discuss this technique. In Loop Rules 2 and 3 (of Section 5.1) we will see a kind of augmentation that involves adding a "sentinel node" to a data structure.

Bob Sproull [1981b] describes a powerful kind of data structure augmentation that is referred to as "hints" by researchers at Xerox Palo Alto Research Center. Sproull describes them as follows:

> The idea is to have a robust but possibly slow algorithm that always yields the truth, and to include (usually in the data structure) hints that allow a much faster algorithm to work if the hints are accurate; obviously you need to have a way to validate the hint. Hints use several data structures to solve a problem: a fast, efficient, but perhaps fragile mechanism is combined with a slow, robust mechanism to obtain the best features of each.

Sproull offers the following example of how one might use hints in a simple mail system.

> Consider a text file that contains a sequence of electronic mail messages in which each message is heralded by the string "------****------". The robust algorithm for finding the ith message or for finding one from a given person is to search the text file, looking for the message heralds, and then to count the message numbers or to parse the header fields, etc. To make this efficient we build a "directory" of the file that includes information about each message, together with a pointer to the character in the file where the message begins. The pointer is a hint; in fact, the entire directory is a hint, because it can be reconstructed from the (original, complete, robust) data structure, the text file. When we follow a pointer, we check that it actually points to the herald string to ensure that the directory pointed to the right place in the file; moreover, we can check the header fields against the directory, etc. These checks validate the hint. If the hint is found to be invalid, we can use the robust algorithm to find the appropriate message, and can (optionally) rebuild the damaged directory.

Lampson and Sproull [1979] describe in detail how hints were used throughout the file system of the Alto personal computer.

The next tradeoff is perhaps the one used most commonly with the greatest savings in time.

> **Space-For-Time Rule 2—Store Precomputed Results:** The cost of recomputing an expensive function can be reduced by computing the function only once and storing the results. Subsequent requests for the function are then handled by table lookup rather than by computing the function.

We already saw a simple application of this rule as we changed Fragment A1 to A2 by computing the distance between points only once and storing it in the variable ThisDist. Peterson [1975] used this technique to avoid re-evaluation of board positions in a game-playing program by storing the value of each board position the program ever evaluated; this reduced the run time on a 3-by-5 board from 27.10 seconds to 0.18 seconds. Bird [1980] discusses storing precomputed results in the general context of recursive programs.

We will consider an application of this rule to a program that repeatedly computes Fibonacci numbers, which are recursively defined as

$$\text{Fib}(1) = 1, \text{Fib}(2) = 1, \text{and}$$
$$\text{Fib}(N) = \text{Fib}(N-1) + \text{Fib}(N-2) \text{ for } N > 2.$$

The first eight Fibonacci numbers are 1, 1, 2, 3, 5, 8, 13, and 21. It is easy to translate the above recursive definition into the Pascal-like subroutine of Fragment B1.

```
function Fib(N: integer): integer;
  var A, B, C, I: integer;
  begin
  if N<1 or N>MaxFib then return 0;
  if N<=2 then return 1;
  A := 1;  B := 1;
  for I := 3 to N do
    begin
    C := A + B;
    A := B;
    B := C
    end;
  return C
  end;
```

Fragment B1. Fibonacci numbers.

Subroutine Fib returns 0 if its input parameter N is less than 1 or greater than the upper limit Max (this avoids the overflow problem in computing large Fibonacci numbers). If this subroutine were in the time bottleneck of a program, then we could replace it by a table defined as

```
var FibVec:  array [1..MaxFib] of integer;
```

and replace each call of Fib(N) by the simple access to FibVec[N], assuming that we have ensured that N is in the range 1..MaxFib. (We will return to this problem when we study Space-For-Time Rule 4.)

Stu Feldman [1981] used this technique in a program to calculate the number of ones in each word in a long series of 23-bit binary codewords. A simple program to accomplish this task would have required over a week of computer time. Feldman's program stored the codewords in 32-bit words and calculated the desired value by adding together the number of ones in three eight-bit fields. To calculate each of those values the program used the eight-bit field as an index into a precomputed 256-element table of integers in which the ith element contained the number of ones in the binary representation of i. The resulting program (which incorporated several other speedups) ran in less than two hours, which was acceptable for a single-shot weekend run.

The next rule is an extension of the previous rule that has many applications throughout computer science.

Space-For-Time Rule 3—Caching: Data that is accessed most often should be the cheapest to access.

This rule is used in computer hardware, for instance, by having a cache in the memory system that stores words that have been recently accessed. When a request arrives for a particular word, the memory system first checks to see if the desired word is in the cache; if the word is there then it can be returned immediately, without the need for the costly address mapping and access to main memory. The same idea is used in searching sequential lists by moving each item as it is found closer to the front of the list; items that are retrieved often tend to be near the front of the list, so they are found quickly (see Knuth [1973, Section 6.1]). Jalics [1977, p. 140] describes an application in which caching the last item retrieved from a table was sufficient to answer 99% of the queries and reduced the cost of answering those queries from 2004 instructions to 4 instructions. Van Wyk's storage allocator described in Section 3.3 is another example of caching: he caches the most commonly used kind of node and uses a general scheme for the rest. Many storage allocators cache common sizes of nodes; Peter Deutsch [1981] reports that when the Smalltalk storage allocator was modified to cache nodes the size of activation records, the run time of many Smalltalk programs decreased by thirty percent.

For another example of caching, consider the problem of implementing a computerized dictionary used to ensure that every word in a manuscript file is indeed in the dictionary. The huge size of the language (some dictionaries contain half a million words) dictates that most words must be stored in secondary memory, but caching (for instance) the one thousand most frequently used English words in main memory would make accesses to the secondary store rare for many documents. A strategy similar to this was used by Peterson [1980] in a spelling correction program.

The following note from Rick Cattell [1981] describes how a database system at Xerox Palo Alto Research Center uses caching.

Our database system keeps the type information about data in the database as data like any other data. This isn't just because this is more elegant; it also makes the user/program interface simpler because the same primitives can be used to access the type tuples as the data tuples. Unfortunately, if this is implemented in the obvious way it turns out that each primitive operation, such as retrieving a field of a tuple, takes eight (!) similar accesses to fields of type tuples to do the type determination and checking. Because most database applications only deal with a few types of tuples, fields, and indexes, I implemented a cache that keeps information on the last twenty type tuples accessed. This entirely avoids the extra eight accesses and the table lookup and checks are a small number of microseconds. The result sped up our most primitive operation, GetField, from 8 milliseconds to about 1.4 milliseconds. Other optimizations, such as caching certain information about types and writing some primitive operations in line instead of procedure calls, reduced the time to about 0.7 milliseconds.

We will discuss writing operations in line in Procedure Rule 1.

Caching can sometimes backfire and actually increase the run time of a program. Caching pays a price to check the cache in hopes that it will find the desired element and thereby avoid a more expensive operation. If the item is not often found in the cache, then the cost of checking might be greater than the benefit of sometimes avoiding the more expensive operation.

The next rule is often used in conjunction with Space-For-Time Rule 2 (Storing Precomputed Results).

Space-For-Time Rule 4—Lazy Evaluation: The strategy of never evaluating an item until it is needed avoids evaluations of unnecessary items.

This rule counters the well-known proverb by advising the programmer to "never do today what you can put off until tomorrow". For a simple example of lazy evaluation, we will return to the problem of computing Fibonacci numbers that we studied in Space-For-Time Rule 2. We saw that a subroutine that computes a Fibonacci number can be replaced by a program that first computes all possible desired numbers and then stores them all in a table. This technique, though, does unneeded work if we never access more than the first few Fibonacci numbers. Fragment B2 reduces the cost of initially evaluating all possible numbers by evaluating each number once and only once, *as it is needed*.

```
function Fib(N: integer): integer;
   var I: integer;
   static TopGood: integer (initially 2);
          GoodFibs: array [1..MaxFib] of integer
                               (initially [1,1]);
   begin
   if N<1 or N>MaxFib then return 0;
   if N>TopGood then
     begin
     for I := TopGood+1 to N do
       GoodFibs[I] :=
           GoodFibs[I-1] + GoodFibs[I-2];
       TopGood := N
     end;
   return GoodFibs[N]
   end;
```

Fragment B2.   Lazy evaluation of Fibonacci numbers.

In the above fragment the static[1] variables TopGood and GoodFibs have the invariant relation that GoodFibs[1..TopGood] always contains the first TopGood Fibonacci numbers, and later elements of the array GoodFibs are undefined.

To illustrate more subtle applications of lazy evaluation, we will consider two examples. The first was supplied by Al Aho [1980], who had constructed an efficient table-driven program to locate a given pattern in a long string.[2] The size of the table was a fast growing function of the length of pattern, but after the table had been built, the string could be processed quickly. Unfortunately, on some inputs his program spent approximately thirty seconds merely building the table. When he replaced that by a lazy evaluation of the table (that is, his program evaluated each table element as it was needed), the run time of the entire program was less than half a second.

A second application of lazy evaluation was described by Brian Kernighan [1981]. When he monitored the TROFF program (a Unix® document formatter), he found that approximately twenty percent of the run time of the program was devoted to calculating the width of the current line after each input

---

[1]The static variables in this procedure are not part of standard Pascal, but can be found in many languages. The declaration static TopGood: integer (initially 2); creates the variable TopGood that is local to this procedure, has the initial value of two, and retains its value between calls. The declaration of GoodFibs creates a local array unchanged between calls whose first two elements are initially 1.

[2]In technical terms, the pattern was specified by a regular expression, and the table represented a deterministic finite-state automaton.

character, and also observed that the width was rarely accessed. He therefore changed the program to store the current line, and calculated the width from that representation on the few occasions when the width was needed. This change was easy to incorporate into the program, and reduced its run time by twenty percent.

4.2 TRADING TIME FOR SPACE

We will now study two techniques that decrease a program's space requirements;[3] they both trade time for space by recomputing information from compact representations.

> **Time-For-Space Rule 1—Packing:** Dense storage representations can decrease storage costs by increasing the time required to store and retrieve data.

The classical example of packing is the representation of integers. On the IBM System/360-370, for example, integers stored as character strings require eight bits per decimal digit, but can be read from and written to external media without change. The "packed decimal" format requires four bits per digit, while a binary representation requires only approximately 3.3 bits per decimal digit. These three representations illustrate three levels of packing: none at all, an intermediate level, and an optimal packing.

For a more sophisticated example of packing we will consider a data structure that arose in a geopolitical database. The bulk of main storage of the (512K 16-bit word) computer was devoted to storing a collection of approximately 10,000 records, each of which contained 36 integers. Upon inspection we found that the vast majority (over 99%) of records had all 36 fields in the range 0..1000. We could therefore use only 10 bits to store each integer in all of those records, which allowed us to put three integers in two 16-bit words, and reduce the size of the record from 36 to 24 words. The few records with greater integers were marked with a flag and stored in the old format. This method greatly increases the time required to access each integer (because accessing a particular integer requires shifting and masking bits off), but reduces the storage requirement to about two thirds of its previous size. The method wasn't implemented because the system's storage stayed within bounds, but its existence was of great psychological comfort as the system grew close to the size limit.

The literature contains many variants on the basic theme of packing. Peterson [1979] and Reghbati [1981] survey a number of packing techniques. Peterson [1980, pp. 56 ff.] represents a dictionary in little space by using radix-40 packing to store three alphanumeric characters in one 16-bit word.

---

[3]Brooks [1975, Chapter 9] discusses several techniques for decreasing space; in particular, he points out that program space can usually be reduced by decreasing functionality.

Morris [1978] shows that one can count large numbers of events in small registers by trading accuracy for space. Knuth [1968, Exercise 2.2.4-18] describes a kind of packing that allows a linked list with a single pointer per node to be traversed either front-to-back or back-to-front. Knuth [1973] uses packing to represent a set of primes succinctly (on page 401) and to compress text (on page 444 and in Exercise 6.3-42).

A common application of packing is to pack data in files on secondary storage. This method decreases the storage required by the file, the input-output time required to read and write files, and the processing time required to translate the data between internal and external format. Applying this technique, John Laird [1981] found that by storing a data structure of floating point numbers in a packed binary format he was able to read it 80 times faster than when it was stored in character representation. (This was due partly to the decreased input/output cost from fewer bytes being read but primarily to less computation for translating from one representation to the other.)

When we pack data we decrease the space required to store the data by increasing both the time required to access it and the space to store the program that manipulates it. Stu Feldman [1981] observed this in a space-critical FORTRAN 77 compiler on a PDP-11, in which he had packed the elements of several kinds of records into four-bit fields. When he unpacked the records (by storing the fields in eight-bit bytes) he found that the code space was reduced by over four thousand bytes (out of 65,000), while the data space increased just slightly. Thus the several extra masking and shifting instructions used by each code fragment that accessed the records required more code space than the data space they saved.

Overlaying is a kind of packing that decreases data space by increasing the difficulty of maintaining the code. The underlying idea is to let data items that are not used at the same time reside in the same space in memory. This idea is supported in FORTRAN by EQUIVALENCE statements, and in Pascal by variant records. Fragments A4 through A7 of Chapter 2 offer an opportunity for overlaying if the program must produce an output vector that contains the points in the order of their nearest neighbor tour. A simple implementation would use a separate output vector and store each point as it was selected. A more sophisticated version could observe that after J points have been visited, UnVis[NumPts$-J+1$..NumPts] contains the J visited points in order (the first city visited is rightmost in the array). Thus when the program is finished, UnVis contains the tour in reverse order. This program overlays in one physical vector two logical vectors: the left part of UnVis contains the unvisited cities in an arbitrary order, and the right part contains the visited cities in reverse order. This program uses one less vector (and therefore half as much extra memory) than the straightforward version, but it is more subtle, and therefore potentially more difficult to debug and to maintain.

Overlaying can be used to reduce code space by organizing a program to keep in primary memory only routines that are currently needed, while keeping the remainder of the routines in a secondary memory. When a new routine is needed, it is overlayed in a portion of storage that holds a routine that is no longer needed. Explicitly structuring a set of routines in this fashion can be tedious, and many operating systems provide this facility as part of a virtual memory system. This decreases program space by increasing the time required to load code from secondary storage.

The final data structure rule that we will examine reduces not the data structure space of a program, but rather the space devoted to storing the program itself.

> **Time-For-Space Rule 2—Interpreters:** The space required to represent a program can often be decreased by the use of interpreters in which common sequences of operations are represented compactly.

This rule is applied in the development of all large systems, with the motivation not of producing space-efficient code but rather of producing understandable code; this is the idea underlying the refinement of a program into subroutines. If we have an action that is done in many different parts of the program (perhaps with some minor changes), we describe it once as a subroutine and then call it many times (perhaps with parameters to describe the changes). This use of subroutines decreases the storage cost of the program by slightly increasing the time cost through the procedure call mechanism and the generality of parameters; we will see in Section 5.3 that these costs can often be avoided, if necessary.

There are many examples of more complex interpreters. It is typical, for instance, to perform the lexical analysis of a program text by a finite state machine (FSM). Although an FSM can be implemented directly in a programming language with either `while` loops or `goto`'s, they are often easier to implement by a small FSM interpreter (less than a dozen lines of code) that executes the FSM defined in a two-dimensional table. Although the table-driven interpreter is minutely slower than a directly-coded FSM, it offers many advantages: it is easier to define, to code, to prove correct, and to maintain, and it usually requires less memory. For details on this approach, see, for instance, Wulf, Shaw, Hilfinger, and Flon [1981, Chapters 1 and 19]. Brooks [1975, pp. 102-103] describes the following applications of interpreters:

> I recall a young man undertaking to build an elaborate console interpreter for an IBM 650. He ended up packing it onto an incredibly small amount of space by building an interpreter for the interpreter, recognizing that human interactions are slow and infrequent, but space was dear. Digitek's elegant little FORTRAN compiler uses a very dense, specialized representation for the compiler code itself, so that external storage is not needed. That time lost in decoding this representation is gained back tenfold by avoiding input-output.

For an excellent general discussion of the applications and construction of interpreters, see Knuth [1968, Section 1.4.3]. Jackson [1975, Section 12.8] describes an application of interpreters in business data processing.

Interpreters arise in many other aspects of programming. Kernighan and Plauger [1978, pp. 48-49] advise us to "use data arrays to avoid repetitive control sequences"; this gives cleaner code that is usually more space-efficient. The machine code provided by the underlying computer architecture can be a useful interpreter in some applications. For instance, in system sorting routines the user gives a (possibly complex) specification of when one record is to precede another. It would be very time consuming to refer to such a specification each time two records are compared, so many sorting routines compile the specifications into code and then pass control to the code to compare two records. This messy approach of compiling tables into machine code is occasionally useful to exploit the full potential of the underlying machine.

4.3 OTHER DATA STRUCTURE MODIFICATIONS

In this chapter we have seen a number of ways of trading space and time against each other. Although the descriptions in this section were in particular directions (time for space or space for time), they can all be applied in the opposite direction also. The following is a brief summary of the opposite directions of the tradeoffs:

- **Space-For-Time Rule 1′—Data Structure Reduction:** Remove unneeded fields from data structures (such as excess pointers and unpacked fields). Packing (Time-For-Space Rule 1) is a special case of this rule.

- **Space-For-Time Rule 2′—Recompute Results:** Instead of storing results, recompute them from scratch. In the early days of computing it was common to store tables of common arithmetic functions such as sine and cosine; those functions are now computed as needed.

- **Space-For-Time Rule 3′—Uncaching:** If locality is not present in a program, explicit caching will still cost space (for the cache) and time (for checking whether the given item is in the cache) but will yield little speedup. A more general application of uncaching conserves space by storing rarely used data in a (large and slow) secondary memory rather than in a (small and fast) primary memory.

- **Space-For-Time Rule 4′—Eager Evaluation:** By evaluating an entire table before it is needed we can avoid the time and space required to check if a particular element has already been evaluated.

- **Time-For-Space Rule 1′—Unpacking:** This is a special case of Space-For-Time Rule 1.

- **Time-For-Space Rule 2′—Compilation to Code:** By writing procedure bodies in line we avoid the overhead of procedure calls; see Procedure Rule 1 (Collapsing Procedure Hierarchies).

4.4 EXERCISES

4.1. Suppose that a program implements a sequence of 1000 records as a singly-linked list; Fragment G1 in Section 5.1 describes such a data structure. Describe how you would increase the speed of the program if monitoring revealed the following facts:

   a. Most of the time is spent in sequentially searching from the front of the list to find the predecessor of the current element.

   b. Most of the time is spent in sequentially searching from the front of the list for an element not more than a few nodes away from the current element.

   c. Most of the time is spent in sequentially searching from the front of the list for the element at the end of the list.

4.2. Describe several implementations of a subroutine named DayOfWeek that is given a date in the 1900's specified by month, day, and year (from 01/01/00 to 12/31/99) and returns the day of the week of that day as an integer in 1..7. Describe the various levels of precomputing suitable in such a subroutine, ranging from using just a dozen words of excess storage to many thousands of words. Which levels are practical?

4.3. In Space-For-Time Rule 3 (Caching) we considered the problem of storing a computerized English dictionary to be used in a spelling-checking program. The approach we studied proposed caching the one thousand most frequently used words in main memory, which is effective for dealing with words common to many documents. In most documents, though, certain words occur frequently that do not occur in most files (for instance, the words "time", "space", and "program" each account for more than one percent of the words in this chapter, but occur infrequently in most text). How would you augment the caching scheme described earlier to cache also the common words in the particular document being examined?

4.4. The following problem arose in a data-entry program written in BASIC to run on a personal computer system. The inner loop of the program read a character from the keyboard and displayed that character on the screen. Because the screen was 64 characters wide while the data was displayed in 50-character rows, an important part of the inner loop was to convert the integer $50I+J$ to the integer $C+64I+J$, where $1 \leqslant J \leqslant 50$. The typical use of the program performed this conversion on a long sequence of integers (for instance, 1, 2, 3, ..., 100). When I first implemented the program I accomplished this step (roughly) by dividing the input integer by fifty, converting the result to the integer I, multiplying I by fifty and subtracting. I was amazed to find that this led to a program that was so slow that it would sometimes drop input characters because it had not finished processing the current character by the time the next character was available. How can the techniques of this chapter be used to increase the efficiency of the conversion?

4.5. We saw that both Space-For-Time Rule 3 (Caching) and Time-For-Space Rule 1 (Packing) can backfire and actually increase the usage of the scarce resource they were intended to decrease. This fact was only sketched in the chapter; give a quantitative description of how these rules can backfire.

4.6. Consider the problem of producing error messages as a compiler is translating a source language program. A simple approach looks up an internal error number in a table of (number, text) pairs stored in a secondary memory to find the text associated with the error number as each error is discovered. Discuss how Space-For-Time Rules 3 and 4 (Caching and Lazy Evaluation) could be used to decrease the time a compiler spends in processing error messages.

4.7. How many letters (ignoring upper and lower case) can be stored in a 36-bit word? How many decimal digits can be stored in a 16-bit word? Sketch routines for packing and unpacking elements in these dense representations.

4.8. Suppose that we wish to put our computer to the good use of producing customized form letters that assure us that "you and the entire Occupant family will enjoy our new optimizing compiler". A naive approach to this problem is to have some poor programmer write a separate program for each distinct form letter; such a program reads a file of names and addresses and constructs letters with the fields of each record placed in the appropriate parts of a letter. Sketch how a single program that implements an interpreter could remove the need for writing a separate program for each form letter.

4.9. [D. E. Knuth] Suppose that you wanted to store a large library of songs as space-efficiently as possible. An obvious technique to reduce space stores the chorus only once and then inserts a special symbol each time the chorus is to be sung. Discuss other techniques that would allow space to be reduced even further for some songs; be sure to consider such musical classics as "On the Nth day of Christmas" and "N bottles of beer on the wall". Sketch how an interpreter could reconstruct text from these compact encodings.

5

MODIFYING CODE

In this chapter we will study efficiency rules that increase the speed of small pieces of code. The rules make local transformations that are almost independent of the systems on which the code is implemented. That point is important to emphasize: we are not concerned here with the best way to accomplish a particular operation on a particular system. It is a compiler's job to implement a certain computation on a particular architecture; it is our job to give the compiler an efficient initial computation.

This chapter is divided into four sections, each of which discusses efficiency rules that deal with a different type of computation. The four types are loops, logic, procedures, and expressions. Several of the rules appear in slightly altered form in more than one place, so it is important to realize that the classification imposed by the sections is not meant to be absolute, but rather to be a guide for a programmer trying to speed up a particular piece of code.

5.1 LOOP RULES

The efficiency rules used most frequently deal with loops for the simple reason that the hot spots in most programs involve loops. (It is awfully hard for code to take a lot of time if it isn't executed a lot, and the most common—although not the only—way to be executed a lot is to be in a loop.) Our approach in this section will be to study individually six rules that each reduce some particular cost of a loop; at the end of the section we will return to view the six rules as a collection.

The first efficiency rule deals with repeated computation in loops.

Loop Rule 1—Code Motion Out of Loops: Instead of performing a certain computation in each iteration of a loop, it is better to perform it only once, outside the loop.

The reason for this rule is simple: by incurring the cost of the computation just once outside the loop, we avoid incurring it many times inside the loop. We saw this in the transformation from Fragment A4 to Fragment A5: instead of evaluating `PtArr[ThisPt].X` and `PtArr[ThisPt].Y` each time through the loop, we evaluate them only once and store them in the variables `ThisX` and `ThisY`. A similar but more substantial savings can be achieved in the following program, whose purpose is to multiply each element of `X[1..N]` by $e^{\mathrm{sqrt}(pi/2)}$.

```
for I := 1 to N do
  X[I] := X[I] * exp(sqrt(Pi/2))
```
Fragment C1.   Scale elements of an array.

Instead of repeatedly performing the expensive division, square root, and exponentiation each time through the loop, we can perform it only once, as in the following code:

```
Factor := exp(sqrt(Pi/2));
for I := 1 to N do
  X[I] := X[I] * Factor
```
Fragment C2.   Evaluate Factor once outside the loop.

When these two fragments were executed under the Hamburg Pascal compiler described in Appendix A, Fragment C1 required $\sim 138N$ microseconds, while Fragment C2 required only $\sim 7.9N$ microseconds. Fragment C2 is usually faster, and it does not compromise the clarity of the code.

Code cannot be moved out of a loop if it has side effects that are desired every loop. For instance, we would probably be disappointed if our compiler moved the statement `read(X)` out of the input loop of our program on the grounds that the statement did not depend on any loop variables. Although the error in this example is obvious, it is easy to make more subtle errors of this form (especially when procedures have subtle side effects).

Code motion out of loops is easy to implement mechanically, and many compilers already perform this transformation on the code they produce. A programmer should also be aware that this transformation can actually increase the run time of a program by moving code out of a loop that is executed zero times. Baskett [1978] describes a simple way that compilers can avoid this pitfall; we will see an application of that method in the insertion sort program at the end of this section.

The next rule is almost never implemented by a compiler because it involves a real (though usually local) change to the computation performed by the program:

Loop Rule 2—Combining Tests: An efficient inner loop should contain as few tests as possible, and preferably only one. The programmer should therefore try to simulate some of the exit conditions of the loop by other exit conditions.

We used this rule to reduce the cost of termination checking as we transformed Fragment A8 to Fragment A9. An oft-cited application of this rule deals with the following sequential search program.

```
I := 1;
while I <= N cand X[I] <> T do
    I := I+1;
if I <= N then
    (* Successful search: T = X[I] *)
    Found := true
  else
    (* Unsuccessful search: T is not in X[1..N] *)
    Found := false
```

Fragment D1.   Sequential search in an unsorted table.

This program uses McCarthy's conditional and operator abbreviated as cand. To evaluate "A cand B", we first test A and then test B only if A is true. This is necessary to avoid accessing X[N+1] during the last iteration of an unsuccessful search. The last six lines of the program could be replaced by the assignment "Found := I<=N". The program was presented in its current form to facilitate processing the search element after it is found; such processing can replace the assignment "Found := true".

The loop in Fragment D1 searches through the array X looking for the value T, and terminates in one of two ways: it either finds T in X[I], or it runs out of valid values of I to investigate. Although it might seem that these two cases really are distinct and that both must be considered in the loop, the following program cleverly simulates the action of "running out of values" by "finding the desired element".

```
X[N+1] := T;
I := 1;
while X[I] <> T do
    I := I+1;
if I <= N then
    Found := true
  else
    Found := false
```

Fragment D2.   Add sentinel to end of table.

This version of the program is potentially much faster than the previous version: it contains only half as many tests. Under the Hamburg Pascal compiler, Fragment D1 requires $\sim 7.3C$ microseconds while Fragment D2 requires only $\sim 4.1C$

microseconds, where C is the number of comparisons made (note that C is between 1 and $N+1$). This is a time savings of over 45 percent. Knuth [1973, Section 6.1] reports that this change reduces the run time of a carefully coded program in the MIX assembly language from ~$5C$ to ~$4C$ time units, and Knuth [1974, p. 267] reports that the change reduces the number of memory references on a "typical" computer from ~$6C$ to ~$4C$.

Fragment D does have one serious problem, though: what about the old value of X[N+1]? We might have just clobbered an important element of the array, or (even worse), the array X might contain only N elements and we just generated an array index out of bounds. This modification to the program can therefore only be incorporated if we are careful to ensure that the position is indeed valid and modifiable. (Jim Peterson [1981] observes that if X[N+1] exists then we could store X[N+1] in a temporary variable, execute the search, and then restore the variable after the search.) This change therefore increases the program's speed by decreasing its robustness. Precisely this problem led to an insidious bug in code produced by a C compiler for the switch statement (that statement uses a given value to select one of many possible actions to execute). The compiler implemented the statement by scanning a table of (value, routine-address) pairs with a sentinel at the end that represented the default value. Storing the current value into that sentinel location caused the code to be non-reentrant, but the bug surfaced only when the switch statement was interrupted during execution by a different process that itself invoked that same switch, which occurred remarkably infrequently. The bug was fixed by removing the sentinel, and the performance of most C programs was unchanged.

Fragment D2 illustrates a common application of Loop Rule 2 (and Space-For-Time Rule 1—Data Structure Augmentation) to data structures for searching: to avoid testing whether we have exhausted a data structure, we can augment the structure with a *sentinel* at the boundary in which we place the object for which we are searching. In a binary search tree, for instance, we could replace all nil pointers by pointers to a sentinel node. When we search, we first place the search object, T, in the sentinel node and proceed as usual. When we find T we then test whether it was in a real node of the tree or the sentinel node. Knuth [1973] reports in Exercise 6.2.2-3 that this change decreases the run time of a MIX binary search tree program from ~$6.5C$ to ~$5.5C$, where C is the number of comparisons made. He used a similar technique in Exercise 5.2.1-33 to decrease the times of two sorting programs from ~$9B$ to ~$8B$ and from ~$7B$ to ~$6B$, in Exercise 6.4-12 to decrease the run time of a hashing inner loop from ~$5C$ to ~$4C$, and in Exercise 6.1-4 to decrease the run time of searching a linked list. On page 160 Knuth describes how sentinels can be used to make a merge program simpler while slightly increasing its run time. In Fragment A9, the value IntArr[HighPt+1] serves as a sentinel that allows us to remove the comparison of I to HighPt in the for loop of Fragment A8. When implementing many board games, it is common to surround the board with a layer of special cells to make the inner loops simpler and faster. Raphael Finkel [1981] refers to this idea as implanting "pseudo data" in a structure.

Bob Sproull [1981b] described how sentinels were used in the design of a compiler for SAIL (the Stanford Artificial Intelligence Language). The lexical analyzer allocated several 128-word buffers to hold source text that the operating system read directly from disk. After the end of each buffer was a word whose first character was a special character that occurred rarely (but *could* occur) in a SAIL program. The scanner then processed the input stream of characters, and only when it saw the special character did it test whether the buffer was exhausted. This use of a special character as a sentinel removed the test for end-of-buffer from the inner loop to a place where it was executed only rarely.

Loop Rule 2 can be used in many other ways. As an example, we will consider Fragment E1, which performs a sequential search in a sorted table. A lecture I heard claimed that Fragment E1 is more expensive than Fragment D1 (a sequential search in an unsorted table) because the former makes three comparisons per loop (two of X[I] to T and one to implement the for loop), while the latter makes only two.

```
for I := 1 to N do
  begin
  if X[I] = T then
    begin Found := true;  goto Done end;
  if X[I] > T then
    begin Found := false; goto Done end;
  end;
Found := false;
Done:
```

Fragment E1.   Sequential search in a sorted table.

We can immediately notice that the two comparisons made in the begin-end block are similar, and replace them by the statement "if X[I] >= T then goto Done", and set Found accordingly outside the loop. With that change we can also convert the for loop to a while loop, which results in Fragment E2.

```
I := 1;
while I <= N cand X[I] < T do
    I := I+1;
if I <= N cand T = X[I] then
    Found := true
  else
    Found := false
```

Fragment E2.   Combine the two comparisons of T to X[I].

Under the Hamburg Pascal compiler, this change actually *increases* the cost of the computation. Fragment E1 requires $\sim 6.8C$ microseconds (where C is the number of comparisons made) while Fragment D2 requires $\sim 7.3C$ microseconds. This increase is due entirely to the efficient implementation of for loops, and is quite system-dependent. (With array bounds checking enabled, for instance, the Pascal running time of Fragment E1 was ~11.3C microseconds and that of Fragment E2 was ~9.0C microseconds.) Changing Fragment E2 to use the same `for` loop structure as Fragment E1 resulted in a running time of 4.5C microseconds, for a speedup of thirty-three percent.

With the above code it is easy to put a sentinel at the end of the table (just as in Fragment D2), which results in Fragment E3.

```
X[N+1] := T;
I := 1;
while X[I] < T do
    I := I+1;
if I <= N cand T = X[I] then
    Found := true
  else
    Found := false
```

Fragment E3.   Add T to end of table.

Because this is a sorted array, we could have implemented the sentinel by ensuring that the highest possible key value is always at the end of the table. Although Fragment E1 was criticized for making fifty percent more comparisons than Fragment D1, the slightly modified version of Fragment E3 makes only half as many. The Pascal running time of Fragment E3 is ~4.1C microseconds, which is forty percent less than the time of Fragment E1.

Bob Sproull [1981b] described a more sophisticated application of combining tests to increase the speed of a re-display inner loop of a raster graphics screen editor. The logic of the program dictated that the current stream of characters should be displayed until one of the following three conditions was satisfied:

- the text source buffer is depleted,
- the display area on the screen is filled, or
- a font or formatting change should be made.

The obvious implementation would test each of the three conditions inside the main loop. The editor achieved a faster loop by calculating outside the loop the remaining number of characters before each of the conditions was true, and then performing the loop for the minimum number of those three integers. This combined three complicated tests into one simple test, and implemented the guts of the re-display algorithm with a simple counting loop.

The next rule allows us to eliminate some of the overhead in extremely tight loops.

Loop Rule 3—Loop Unrolling: A large cost of some short loops is in modifying the loop indices. That cost can often be reduced by unrolling the loop.

As an example of a loop in which most of the expense is devoted to index over-head, consider Fragment F1, which places in Sum the sum of the elements of X[1..10].

```
Sum : = 0;
for I : = 1 to 10 do
   Sum : = Sum + X[I]
```

Fragment F1. Compute the sum of X[1..10].

In each iteration of the loop there is only one "real" operation (the addition), but there is the overhead of adding 1 to I and comparing I to 10. That overhead is eliminated entirely in the following code.

```
Sum : = X[1] + X[2] + X[3] + X[4] + X[5]
      + X[6] + X[7] + X[8] + X[9] + X[10]
```

Fragment F2. Unrolled sum of X[1..10].

We now have just nine additions and no other loop overhead. Under the Hamburg Pascal compiler, Fragment F1 required 63.4 microseconds while Fragment F2 required just 22.1 microseconds. Loop unrolling often decreases program run times dramatically. When a microcomputer's multiply instruction is implemented in software rather than in hardware, unrolling the main loop can sometimes decrease the subroutine's time by thirty percent. Unrolling is also commonly used in system numerical routines for computing functions such as square root and logarithm. Instead of testing for convergence at each iteration, a numerical analyst can prove that it will take at most k iterations and then unroll the loop k times.

So far we have only discussed unrolling a loop that is executed a constant number of times; the technique can also be extended to general loops that are executed a variable number of times. To unroll such a loop k times, we repeat k copies of the code in the main loop, and then test in the control part whether we are within k of the end of the loop. We must take special care to handle the end values properly. (Jim Peterson [1981] remarks that a common way to implement this in some languages is to jump to the $(N \bmod k)$th repetition from the end, and then do $[N - (N \bmod k)]/k$ complete iterations of the unrolled loop.)

For an example of variable-length loop unrolling, we will return to Fragment E3 (which performs a sequential search in a sorted table). Two operations are performed in each iteration of the loop: T is compared to X[I] and I is incremented by one; thus a large share of the loop's cost is devoted to the unproductive process of incrementing. We decrease that cost in the following code by unrolling the loop five times:[1]

---

[1]In Fragment E4 we use the language construct loop...endloop, which has the semantics of repeating the code it contains in a loop until a break statement is reached, at which time the program resumes execution at the next statement following the loop...endloop. This kind of loop construct is often useful in unrolling loops. If a particular language does not offer this construct, then its effect can be synthesized by disciplined use of goto statements.

```
X[N+1] := T;
I := 1;
loop
    if X[I]   >= T then
      begin Last := I;   break end;
    if X[I+1] >= T then
      begin Last := I+1; break end;
    if X[I+2] >= T then
      begin Last := I+2; break end;
    if X[I+3] >= T then
      begin Last := I+3; break end;
    if X[I+4] >= T then
      begin Last := I+4; break end;
    I := I+5
  endloop;
if Last <= N cand T=X[Last] then
    Found := true
  else
    Found := false
```

Fragment E4.　Loop-unrolled sequential search in a sorted array.

Whereas before we had only one "real" operation (comparing an element of X to T) for every "bookkeeping" operation (adding one to I), we now have a ratio of five real operations for every bookkeeping operation. This reduces the Pascal running time from ~4.1C microseconds to ~3.4C microseconds (a speedup of seventeen percent). This technique can be applied with any value other than five; we trade program size for run time. (One might complain that in the above example we must, for instance, add 3 to I to access X[I+3]; many compilers, though, implement the instruction with 3 as a compiled offset from the base X.) One can use exactly this technique to unroll the inner loop k times in the assembly program A10 of Section 2.3; this would remove the incrementing instruction "LA I,8(I)" from the loop and replace the Load instruction with "L ThisDist,j(I)", where $j=0,8,16,...,(k-1)\cdot 8$. To illustrate the speedups that loop unrolling yields we will consider several additional examples. Knuth [1973] shows in Section 6.1 that unrolling a sequential search loop k times decreases its MIX run time from ~4C to ~$(3+1/k)C$, where C is the number of comparisons made. In Exercise 6.2.1-11, Knuth uses unrolling to reduce the run time of a uniform binary search of an N-element table from ~8.5 $\log_2 N$ to ~4.5 $\log_2 N$. Dongarra and Hinds [1979] present empirical timings that show that unrolling extremely tight FORTRAN loops on high-performance machines can increase their speed by a factor of up to two. Sedgewick [1975, Appendix A] uses loop unrolling to reduce the MIX time of a Quicksort implementation from ~10.63 N ln N to ~9.57 N ln N (see also Sedgewick [1978]).

All of the loops that we have seen so far have the property that the maximum number of iterations is known before the first iteration (some were known even at compile time). We will now consider a different kind of example: taking the sum of a linked list of integers. If we use the standard representation of linked lists, then the loop must access the next node of the list and compare it to `nil` for each addition. Although we cannot remove the cost of accessing the next node, we can reduce the cost of comparison to `nil` by augmenting the list with a special sentinel node at the end. That node has the value of zero and a link field that points to the node itself; we then unroll the loop k times, and test whether we are at the sentinel node every k iterations. We might make up to k unnecessary iterations of the loop, but adding zero to the sum will not change the final result. A "self-pointing" sentinel can be used in other applications to unroll loops whose lengths are unknown at the start of their execution.

We turn now to a special kind of loop unrolling whose purpose is not to reduce the cost of indexing but rather to remove trivial assignments (that is, assignments of the form `I:=J`, where I and J are both simple variables).

Loop Rule 4—Transfer-Driven Loop Unrolling: If a large cost of an inner loop is devoted to trivial assignments, then those assignments can often be removed by repeating the code and changing the use of variables. Specifically, to remove the assignment `I:=J`, the subsequent code must treat J as though it were I.

The name of the rule represents the fact that the way we unroll the loop is driven by the data transfers contained in the loop. The above statement of this rule is vague; we will now illustrate its use by studying two examples in detail. The reader interested in a more detailed study of this technique is referred to the fascinating paper of Mont-Reynaud [1976].

As our first example of transfer-driven unrolling, we will again consider Fragment B1, which computes Fibonnaci numbers. Recall that the program's only loop consists of a `for` statement that contains one assignment (involving an addition) and two trivial assignments. We can remove both of those trivial assignments by modifying the code as shown in Fragment B3.

```
function Fib(N:integer):integer;
  var A,B,I: integer;
  begin
  if N < 1 or N > MaxFib then return 0;
  if N <= 2 then return 1;
  A := 1; B := 1;
  for I := 1 to (N div 2) - 1 do
    begin
    A := A+B;
    B := B+A
    end;
  if odd(N) then
    B := B+A;
  return B
  end;
```

Fragment B3.   Loop-unrolled Fibonacci numbers.

The invariant condition of the loop is that before the first assignment is executed, A contains the $2I-1^{st}$ Fibonacci number and B contains the $2I^{th}$; it is easy to prove the program correct using that invariant. While Fragment B1 used a loop control and two trivial assignments for every "real" operation of addition, Fragment B3 involves only half a loop test for every addition, and that fraction can be reduced by loop unrolling. Under the Hamburg Pascal compiler, Fragment B1 requires 273 microseconds to compute Fib(40), while Fragment B3 requires 143 microseconds; the latter is almost twice as fast as the former.

The second example of transfer-driven unrolling inserts a new node named ThisNode into a sorted linked list whose elements contain both a Link and Value field.[2]To ease programming (and, incidentally, to increase the speed of the loop), we will assume that the list has been augmented to contain sentinel nodes at the head and tail whose values are, respectively, less than and greater than all keys. The code for inserting ThisNode into the list pointed to by Anchor is shown in Fragment G1.

---

[2]The symbol P⌂.Link denotes the Link field of the list node pointed to by the pointer P; similarly, P⌂.Value denotes the Value field of the node.

```
P := Anchor;
Q := P⌂.Link;
while Q⌂.Value <= ThisNode⌂.Value do
  begin
  P := Q;
  Q := Q⌂.Link
  end;
ThisNode⌂.Link := Q;
P⌂.Link := ThisNode
```

Fragment G1.   Insert ThisNode in a sorted linked list.

This is a standard operation on linked lists in which P is always one step behind Q. A substantial percentage of the time in the inner loop is devoted to the trivial assignment "P: =Q". That can be removed by unrolling the loop two times and changing the roles of the variables so that they "leap frog" over one another, first Q in front of P and then P in front of Q. This modification is reflected in Fragment G2.

```
P := Anchor;
loop
  Q := P⌂.Link;
  if Q⌂.Value <= ThisNode⌂.Value then
    begin
    ThisNode⌂.Link := Q;
    P⌂.Link := ThisNode;
    break
    end
  P := Q⌂.Link;
  if P⌂.Value <= ThisNode⌂.Value then
    begin
    ThisNode⌂.Link := P;
    Q⌂.Link := ThisNode;
    break
    end
endloop
```

Fragment G2. Remove trivial assignment.

This code makes only one assignment (involving a Link field) and one test for each node visited; Fragment G1 involved an extra trivial assignment statement.

To illustrate the impact of transfer-driven loop unrolling we will again turn to several well-coded MIX programs of Knuth [1973]. In Exercise 5.2.1-33 he shows that a change similar to unrolling Fragment G1 to achieve G2 reduces the MIX time from $\sim 6B$ to $\sim 5B$. Exercise 5.2.4-15 reduces the time of a merge sort from $\sim 10N \log_2 N$ to $\sim 8N \log_2 N$, and on page 426 he reduces the time of a binary tree search from $\sim 7.5C$ to $\sim 6.5C$. The application of this technique to

Fibonaccian search can be found on pp. 415 and 416. Knuth [1971, p. 124] uses this technique to increase the speed of a binary search on an IBM System/360 by a factor of more than 2. Other instances of this technique can be found in Knuth [1968]: Exercise 1.1-3 increases the efficiency of the Euclidean algorithm, and Exercise 2.2.3-8 reduces the time to reverse a linked list in place from ~7N time units to ~5N units.

We will now study an efficiency rule that is not appropriate for programs in a high-level language, but can often be used to speed up an inner loop in assembly code or in unstructured languages such as BASIC and FORTRAN.

Loop Rule 5—Unconditional Branch Removal: A fast loop should contain no unconditional branches. An unconditional branch at the end of a loop can be removed by "rotating" the loop to have a conditional branch at the bottom.

As an example of this rule, we will consider the typical low-level implementation of the statement "while C do S" shown in Fragment H1.

```
Loop:   if not C then goto End;
        S;
        goto Loop;
End:
```

Fragment H1. Typical translation of "while C do S".

If the code for C and S is small, then the cost of the unproductive goto can be a substantial amount of the time spent in the loop. That cost is removed in the following fragment:

```
        goto Test;
Loop:   S;
Test:   if C then goto Loop;
End:
```

Fragment H2. Efficient translation of "while C do S".

This translation contains a new unconditional goto outside the loop but has no unconditional branch within the loop (it also avoids inverting the value of C, which saves time in some implementations). This transformation can be applied to loops other than while; for more details on this transformation, see Baskett [1978]. Knuth [1973] uses this technique in all of the inner loops in his text; a particularly interesting example can be found in the organization of Program 6.2.2T.

The above rule usually need not and should not be applied in a high-level language—many compilers recognize loop constructs and compile them very efficiently. By "optimizing" the code one runs the risk that the compiler will not recognize the loop; this change can therefore lead to a slower and more obscure program. When applied to a small loop in a low-level language, though, this technique can often reduce run time by ten or twenty percent.

The next loop rule that we will see is based on the same idea as car-pooling: if two sets of operations work on the same set of values, then why shouldn't they share the ride through those values?

Loop Rule 6—Loop Fusion: If two nearby loops operate on the same set of elements, then combine their operational parts and use only one set of loop control operations.

The application of this rule reduces the loop overhead without impairing the "real" computation that is being performed. It can often be used when two nearby loops operate on the same data structure for unrelated purposes, at the price of confusing the code. For instance, a straightforward program to find both the maximum and minimum elements of an array might iterate through the array twice; a more efficient approach would iterate through the array just once (we will return to this problem in Expression Rule 4—Pairing Computation).

So far we have viewed the efficiency rules for loops in isolation; we will now take a moment to view the rules as a collection. The following list gives the number and name of each of the rules, and briefly describes what unnecessary computation it eliminates from loops:

1. **Code motion out of loops:** eliminates repeated computation.
2. **Combining tests:** reduces the number of tests.
3. **Loop unrolling:** reduces costs of indexing.
4. **Transfer-driven unrolling:** reduces the number of trivial assignments.
5. **Unconditional branch removal:** removes the unconditional branch at the bottom of the loop.
6. **Loop fusion:** shares the cost of loop overhead.

Each individual rule eliminates a different kind of unnecessary computation, and together they can eliminate almost all excess baggage from a loop. We will see in Logic Rule 2 (Short-circuiting Monotone Functions) a technique for eliminating unnecessary iterations of loops, and in Expression Rule 2 (Exploit Algebraic Identities) a technique for simplifying the kind of computation in loops (by strength reduction and induction variable elimination).

As an example of how the above six rules work together on a single loop, we will consider the insertion sorting program for arranging the elements of an array in nondecreasing order shown in Fragment I1. The algorithm works by successively inserting the Ith element into its proper place among the first through the $I-1$st for each I from 2 to N. (For more information on insertion sorting, see Knuth [1973, Section 5.2.1] or Sedgewick [1975, Chapter 1]).

```
for I := 2 to N do
  begin
  J := I;
  while J > 1 cand X[J] < X[J-1] do
    begin
    Swap(X[J],X[J-1]);
    J := J-1
    end
  end
```

Fragment I1.   Insertion sort.

The above program is easy to read and prove correct; in most applications, it should be left in exactly the above state. The fragment has a running time of $\sim 6.00N^2$ microseconds. If sorting is in the program's time bottleneck, though, and this is the best sorting procedure to use (as it is for small values of N), then we are justified in devoting a great deal of energy to improving the program.

The first improvement we should make is to write the call of the Swap procedure in line, which results in the following fragment:

```
for I := 2 to N do
  begin
  J := I;
  while J > 1 cand X[J] < X[J-1] do
    begin
    T := X[J];
    X[J] := X[J-1];
    X[J-1] := T;
    J := J-1
    end
  end
```

Fragment I2.   Swap procedure written in line.

We do this both to eliminate the cost of the procedure call and to allow further time reductions; the code now has a running time of $\sim 3.90N^2$ microseconds. We will now try to apply Loop Rule 1 to move repeated computation out of the loop. Careful inspection of the code shows that X[J] is repeatedly stored to and then loaded from the variable T; we can remove those assignments by rewriting the code as shown in Fragment I3.

```
for I : = 2 to N do
  begin
  J : = I;
  T : = X[I];
  while J > 1 cand T < X[J-1] do
    begin
    X[J] : = X[J-1];
    J : = J-1
    end;
  X[J] : = T
  end
```

Fragment I3.   Move operations on T out of loop.

The run time of this program is $\sim 2.73N^2$ microseconds. (A problem with the above code is that if the while loop is usually executed zero times, then this fragment will take longer than Fragment I2; Knuth [1973] shows how this pitfall can be avoided in Exercise 5.2.1-10 and in Program 5.2.2Q, Step 9.)

We will next try to apply Loop Rule 2 and combine tests. The inner while loop contains two tests that can be reduced to one by placing a sentinel in the zero[th] position of the table; the modified code is shown in Fragment I4.

```
X[0] : = MinusInfinity;
for I : = 2 to N do
  begin
  J : = I;
  T : = X[I];
  while T < X[J-1] do
    begin
    X[J] : = X[J-1];
    J : = J-1
    end;
  X[J] : = T
  end
```

Fragment I4.   Add a sentinel at X[0].

The run time of this fragment is $\sim 2.02N^2$ microseconds. The cumulative effect of these three transformations is to speed the program up by a factor of almost three from the $6.00N^2$ microseconds of Fragment I1.[3]

We can still apply further loop rules to this program. Loop Rule 3 (Loop Unrolling) can be used to reduce the cost of the instruction $J := J-1$ by unrolling the loop some fixed number of times; because that change is so straightforward, we will not show it here. Loop Rule 4 (Transfer-Driven Unrolling) is not applicable to this code because it contains no trivial assignments. Likewise, Loop Rule 5 (Removing Unconditional Branches) is not applicable because we are coding in a high-level language, but it would be used in any efficient low-level language implementation of the program.

Loop Rule 6 (Loop Fusion) has an interesting relation to Fragment I4. On the one hand, it appears not to be applicable because there is only one loop in the program. On the other hand, though, we can view it as having been applied already: the two tasks of finding where to place X[I] and then placing it there might logically be divided into two loops, but our code already performs both tasks with the overhead of only one loop.

5.2 LOGIC RULES

In this section we will study rules that decrease the cost of code that is devoted to logic. In particular, these rules deal with efficiency problems that arise when evaluating the program state by making various kinds of tests. They all take a clean piece of code and massage it so that it is less clear but usually more efficient; in other words, they sacrifice clarity and robustness for speed of execution.

The first rule for manipulating logic will arise again in a similar context as Expression Rule 2.

> **Logic Rule 1—Exploit Algebraic Identities:** If the evaluation of a logical expression is costly, replace it by an algebraically equivalent expression that is cheaper to evaluate.

For instance, instead of testing whether "sqr(X) > 0" in an inner loop, we

---

[3]Kernighan and Plauger [1978, pp. 131-133] study an "efficient" interchange sort that was presented in a programming text and show that a simple version of the same algorithm not only requires only half as many lines of FORTRAN code but is also about thirty percent faster on randomly generated data. Their simple program was conceptually somewhere between Fragments I1 and I2; its Pascal transliteration was eight lines long and had a running time of $4.03N^2$ microseconds. Kernighan and Plauger present this as an illustration of the principle to "keep it simple to make it faster". Fragment I4 contains only twelve lines of (relatively simple) code to achieve a speed increase of a factor of two over Kernighan and Plauger's fast program. Although the fact that Fragment I4 is longer and faster than their program might appear to violate the letter of their maxim, that fragment does follow its spirit: the more complex approach to efficiency they describe results in a program that requires thirty percent more time than the simple program, while our approach of applying simple and well understood transformations results in a program that is more than twice as fast.

SEC. 5.2   LOGIC RULES   **67**

could just as easily test "X<>0" (because the square of an integer is greater than zero if and only if that integer is not zero). Similarly, we could use De Morgan's laws to change the test "not A and not B" to "not (A or B)"; the latter might involve one less negation. In general, we could use the techniques of boolean algebra to minimize the work required to evaluate boolean functions. Costs of operations at this level are, however, dependent on the compiler and the underlying machine, so a programmer must be careful that a clever "optimization" along these lines does not fool the compiler into generating slower code.

There are more substantial applications of Logic Rule 1 that will reduce the run times of many programs on most compilers and machines. For instance, in changing Fragment A2 to A3 we used *strength reduction* to remove a square root. In particular, we wished to compute a boolean variable telling whether a new point was closer than the best point so far. Because square root is a monotone increasing function (that is, for nonnegative arguments, x is greater than y if and only if $sqrt(x)$ is greater than $sqrt(y)$) we could remove the square root from the test. This algebraic technique can often be used to avoid a function evaluation when we are concerned only about the relative ordering of a pair of objects (though it can increase bookkeeping). Knuth [1973, Exercise 6.2.1-23] shows how a different algebraic identity can be used to reduce ternary comparisons (those with the three outcomes $<$, $=$, $>$) to binary, and thereby decrease the cost of a single comparison in comparison-based searching algorithms.

The next rule for dealing with logic allows us to avoid unneeded work after we have already gleaned enough information to make a decision.

Logic Rule 2—Short-circuiting Monotone Functions: If we wish to test whether some monotone nondecreasing function of several variables is over a certain threshold, then we need not evaluate any of the variables once the threshold has been reached.

A common application of this rule is in the evaluation of simple boolean formulas. In some languages, for instance, if we wish to evaluate "A and B", we can write "A cand B", which evaluates A and then evaluates B only if A is true. This avoids the evaluation of B if A is false, which can represent a substantial time savings. (In the Ada language, this feature is explicitly called "short-circuit evaluation".) Of course, we cannot avoid the evaluation of B if it has important side effects. For a more sophisticated application of the rule, consider determining whether there are any negative elements in an array of reals. The most naive (and perhaps cleanest) approach sets the boolean FoundNegative originally to false, and then iterates through the array and sets FoundNegative to true whenever it observes that a given real is negative. It is only slightly more work to modify the loop to terminate precisely at that point, because we can then accurately report that the array does contain a negative. (Don Stanat [1981] observes that using a sentinel of a negative number with this approach reduces the two tests of the previous method to one.)

Logic Rule 2 was our basis for transforming Fragment A5 to A6 by calculating the y-distance between a pair of points only after ensuring that their x-distance alone was not sufficient to discard them from consideration. We will now generalize that idea by examining the problem of determining whether the sum of the real numbers in X[1..N] is greater than the given real CutOff; we will assume that the reals in X are known to be positive (in Fragment A6, for instance, the values were squares and therefore nonnegative). A straightforward program for this task is shown in Fragment J1; the boolean variable Greater is true if and only if the sum of the elements of X is greater than CutOff.

```
Sum := 0;
for I := 1 to N do
  Sum := Sum + X[I];
Greater := Sum > CutOff
```

Fragment J1.   Sum first then compare.

If CutOff is usually less than the sum of the first few values of X, then Fragment J2 is a faster means of accomplishing the same task.

```
I := 1;
Sum := 0;
while I <= N and Sum <= CutOff do
  begin
  Sum := Sum + X[I];
  I := I+1
  end;
Greater := Sum > CutOff
```

Fragment J2.   Compare as we sum.

If the cost of comparing Sum to CutOff is relatively high, or if the probability that the loop will be terminated early is relatively low, then Fragment J2 can be slower than Fragment J1. The two fragments are extremes along a spectrum in which we trade the work of additional comparisons for the expected benefits of early termination of the loop. A middle element of that spectrum is shown in Fragment J3, in which we perform two additions for every comparison.

```
I := 1;
Sum := 0;
if odd(N) then
   begin
   I := 2;
   Sum := X[1]
   end;
while I < N and Sum <= CutOff do
   begin
   Sum := Sum + X[I] + X[I+1];
   I := I+2
   end;
Greater := Sum > CutOff
```

Fragment J3.   Add twice for each compare.

Note the careful preprocessing necessary to unroll the above loop. Raphael Finkel [1981] pointed out that the speed of the above loop can be further increased by using sentinels: ensuring that $X[N+1]$ is greater than CutOff allows us to remove the test "$I<N$" from the while loop. We must then have a more sophisticated test after the loop. Don Stanat [1981] observes that if we further ensure that $X[N+2]$ is zero, then we can remove the preprocessing dealing with odd N.

Logic Rule 2 is especially powerful when dealing with loops that evaluate monotone logical functions. It is usually easiest to write such loops so that they iterate over their entire range of values, and they should be written this way originally. If we later find that such a loop is in a time bottleneck of the program, then we can modify it to terminate early, using a loop exiting construct (such as a break statement or even disciplined and documented use of a goto). Depending on where the jump to threshold usually occurs, this technique can save a factor of two or more on loops that evaluate this particular kind of function. This strategy gives us the best of both worlds: all loops in our programs are initially designed with a clean and straightforward structure, and then the critical loops are modified in an understandable way from understandable code (instead of being monuments to extreme cleverness from their beginning).

The next logic rule reduces the running time of a program by rearranging the sequencing of tests.

Logic Rule 3—Reordering Tests: Logical tests should be arranged such that inexpensive and often successful tests precede expensive and rarely successful tests.

This rule has the corollary that when a series of nonoverlapping conditions is sequentially evaluated until one is true, the inexpensive and common conditions should be evaluated first and the expensive and rare conditions should be evaluated last. (Of course, if evaluating some of the conditions has side effects, then we might not be able to reorder the tests.) As an example of this corollary, we will consider Fragment K1, which is a pseudo-Pascal function that returns an integer code that describes the type of the character it was passed.

```
function CharType(X: char): integer;
  begin
  if X = ' ' then return 1
    else if   ('A' <= X and X <= 'I')
           or ('J' <= X and X <= 'R')
           or ('S' <= X and X <= 'Z') then
        return 2
    else if '0' <= X and X <= '9' then return 3
    else if   X = '+' or X = '/' or X = '-'
           or X = ',' or X = '('
           or X = ')' or X = '=' then return 4
    else if X = '*' then return 5
    else if X = '"' then return 6
    else return 7
  end;
```

Fragment K1.   A character recognizer.

Fragment K1 was used to process every character read by a compiler for a FORTRAN-like language on an IBM System/360; the seven integers respectively denote blank, letter, digit, operator, asterisk, quote, and other. (The test for letter is so complicated because of "holes" in the EBCDIC character code.) Although the above presentation is somewhat clearer, the code actually used in the compiler was similar to that shown in Fragment K2.

```
function CharType(X: char): integer;
  begin
  if X = ' ' then return 1
    else if X = '*' then return 5
    else if X = '"' then return 6
    else if '0' <= X and X <= '9' then return 3
    else if    ('A' <= X and X <= 'I')
            or ('J' <= X and X <= 'R')
            or ('S' <= X and X <= 'Z') then
         return 2
    else if   X = '+' or X = '/' or X = '-'
            or X = ',' or X = '('
            or X = ')' or X = '=' then return 4
    else return 7
  end;
```

Fragment K2.   Order of tests changed.

Fragment K2 will be faster than the previous version if there are enough occurrences of asterisks, quotes and digits to merit their earlier testing. For a precise mathematical formulation of this corollary of Logic Rule 3, see Exercise 5.7. Knuth [1973, Program 6.2.2T] orders the tests in a binary search tree program (lines 10 and 11) to reduce its MIX running time from $\sim 7C$ to $\sim 6.5C$.

Logic Rule 3 has many applications other than performing a sequential series of tests; we will see one in Procedure Rule 2 (Exploit Common Cases). This rule also encourages us to place an expensive test inside a cheaper test. In transforming Fragment A8 to Fragment A9, we placed the loop control test inside the necessary test for a new minimum. This was exactly the same idea underlying the sentinels in Loop Rule 2: we push a test for loop control inside a test on the data structure. Knuth [1973, Exercise 5.2.3-18] uses this idea to reduce the MIX running time of a heapsort program from $\sim 16N \log_2 N$ to $\sim 13N \log_2 N$ time units. A more sophisticated kind of placing one test inside another is to perform an expensive yes-no check by first running a cheaper algorithm that usually returns yes or no but sometimes returns maybe—only in the latter case do we have to perform the more expensive test. An example of such an approximate test in a geometric application is given by Bentley, Faust and Preparata [1982]. Nix [1981] describes a similar approach in a program for correcting spelling errors.

Peter Weinberger [1981] used a cheap but effective "shielding" test in a Scrabble program. The most expensive inner loop was given a slice of a board position (a vector of letters and spaces) and a list of words; it had to tell which words in the list could fit in the slice. That expensive computation was usually avoided by keeping for each word in the dictionary a 26-bit vector (stored in a 32-bit word) that told which letters were present in the word. Before the loop was executed, a similar vector was calculated for the pattern slice, telling what letters it contained.   In the inner loop, a word was tested by the expensive routine only if every one bit in the pattern's vector was also on in that word's vector; this test is a single high-level language statement, and required only a few machine-language instructions.   Monitoring two typical Scrabble games showed that of over twelve million words tested with this scheme, less than a hundred thousand had to be tested further.   This scheme uses Reordering Tests (Logic Rule 3), Storing Precomputed Results (Space-For-Time Rule 2), and Word Parallelism (Expression Rule 5).

Logic Rule 4 is an application of Space-For-Time Rule 2 (Store Precomputed Results) to the domain of logic.

Logic Rule 4—Precompute Logical Functions: A logical function over a small finite domain can be replaced by a lookup in a table that represents the domain.

A simple application of this rule can replace the complicated and slow Char-Type procedure of Fragment K2 by the more elegant program of Fragment K3.

```
function CharType(X: char): integer;
  begin
  return TypeTable[ord(X)]
  end;
```

Fragment K3.   Character recognition by table lookup.

This program determines the type of character X simply by looking at the appropriate entry in a 256-element table (the number of characters in the EBCDIC character code); the function ord is used in Pascal to convert a character to its integer rank.   Peterson [1980] used precisely this method to classify letters in a spelling correction program.   This change results in slightly more space (we have less code but a new table), but is much faster; trading that space for time is wise if much time is spent in Fragment K2.   Kernighan [1981] reports that when translating the programs of Kernighan and Plauger [1978] from Ratfor to Pascal, he observed that between 30 and 40 percent of the running time of some of the Pascal programs was spent in character recognition by a subroutine like Fragment K2; almost all of that time is eliminated by code like that in Fragment K3.   In such an application, the 256-element table would be well worth its space.

Logic Rule 4 has many faces.   Sometimes we use it to replace a long chain of if-then-else-if-then-else statements by a single case statement; clever compilers then choose an optimal implementation of the case statement in the assembly code, and often generate a table.   Knuth [1968, Exercise 1.3.2-9] describes how assembly language coders can implement multiway branches effectively as a jump table.   He uses that technique in Exercise 1.3.2-9 to test for validity of a certain field of an assembly code instruction, in Exercise 1.3.2-23 to prepare graphical output, and on pp. 200-204 to implement an interpreter.[4] If we were evaluating a function of six boolean variables, we could replace the function evaluation by a lookup in a sixty-four (that is, 2^6) element table.

A powerful application of this technique was used by David Moon [1981] in a PDP-8 simulator (which was designed to run on a PDP-10 but was never implemented). Because the PDP-8's memory words are just twelve bits wide, there are only 2^{12}, or 4096, different instructions. Moon observed that instead of interpreting each instruction at run time, he could precompute the actions of all possible instructions, and store them in a 4096-element table of PDP-10 instructions. This led to an extremely efficient inner loop in the simulator: it executes a single instruction, using the current instruction (pointed to by the program counter) as an index into the instruction table. Most of the PDP-8 instructions could be emulated by a single PDP-10 instruction, and those that could not had a subroutine call in their position in the table.

In the final logic rule we will see how the time required to read and write boolean variables can be eliminated by "storing them in the program counter".

Logic Rule 5—Boolean Variable Elimination: We can remove boolean variables from a program by replacing the assignment to a boolean variable V by an if—then—else statement in which one branch represents the case that V is true and the other represents the case that V is false. (This generalizes to case statements and other logical control structures.)

As an instance of the above rule, we will consider Fragment L1, in which we assume the statement S1 changes some variables in LogicalExp.

```
V : = LogicalExp;
S1;
if V then
    S2
  else
    S3
```

Fragment L1.   Code with boolean variable V.

We could replace the above example by the code in Fragment L2, as long as the boolean variable V is used nowhere else in the program.

---

[4]See especially the paragraph starting at the bottom of page 200 and the first sentence on page 204.

```
if LogicalExp then
    begin
    S1;
    S2
    end
else
    begin
    S1;
    S3
    end
```

Fragment L2.   Boolean variable V removed.

The resulting code is larger by the size of S1 (because S1 is now repeated), but is slightly faster.   Knuth [1974, pp. 285-286] shows how boolean variable elimination can be used in the partitioning phase of a Quicksort program to reduce the total run time by about 25 percent.   Knuth [1973, Program 6.2.3A] uses a similar technique to eliminate a variable over $\{-1,0,1\}$ in a program for manipulating balanced binary search trees.

Logic Rule 5 is important for programmers who use boolean variables to synthesize advanced control structures.   For instance, in Fragment D1 (a simple sequential search in an unsorted array), we used a cand statement to avoid accessing X[N+1].   If the language had not provided the cand statement, then many programmers would have solved the problem with code like Fragment D3.

```
X[N+1] := T;
I := 1;
KeepGoing := true;
while KeepGoing do
    if I > N then
        KeepGoing := false
      else if X[I] = T then
        KeepGoing := false
      else
        I := I+1;
if I <= N then
    Found := true
  else
    Found := false
```

Fragment D3.   Fragment D1 implemented with a Boolean variable.

While Fragment D1 requires $7.3C$ microseconds (where C is the number of comparisons of T to elements of X), Fragment D3 requires $7.4C$ microseconds.   If a language does not have a cand statement, then Fragment D3 could be efficiently implemented either by disciplined use of goto statements or by ensuring that no harm will come from accessing $X[N+1]$ (I used the latter approach in Fragment D1); both of those approaches are advanced applications of Boolean Variable Elimination.

A broader application of Logic Rule 5 reorganizes programs to remove boolean variables. Consider a program that iterates through a list in which each element selects an operation on one of the two arrays A and B; a simple implementation would use a boolean variable in each element to decide to which array each operation applies. A more sophisticated program could eliminate the boolean variables by storing the operations on A and on B in separate lists and then using two loops (each without tests) to process the operations.

5.3 PROCEDURE RULES

So far in this chapter we have improved the efficiency of a program by making local changes to small pieces of code. In this section we will take a different approach by leaving the code alone and instead modifying the underlying structure of the program as it is organized into procedures.

The first procedure rule that we will study is the dual of Time-For-Space Rule 2 (Interpreters); we pay in program space to buy run time.

> **Procedure Rule 1—Collapsing Procedure Hierarchies:** The run times of the elements of a set of procedures that (nonrecursively) call themselves can often be reduced by rewriting procedures in line and binding the passed variables.

The simplest application of this rule is that subroutine calls in time bottlenecks should be written in line; this is exactly the method we used in transforming Fragment A4 to A5. This achieves two kinds of savings: we avoid the cost overhead of the procedure call and we often open the way for further optimizations (as in Fragments I2 and I3 of Section 5.1). Stankovich [1979] has studied the general operation of increasing the performance of structured systems by what he refers to as "vertically migrating" expensive operations to be lower in the procedure hierarchy; he describes both a general methodology and its application to a large system. A system-dependent application of collapsing procedure hierarchies is to push common operations in a system down into the operating system, microcode, or even special-purpose hardware. This is difficult to accomplish in most systems, but it can sometimes yield substantial time reductions.

Many languages provide means whereby certain subroutines are always expanded in line (as opposed to being invoked through a subroutine call); this mechanism goes under names such as macros and in-line procedures. Scheifler [1977] studies the benefit this operation can have in entire programs, and asserts that "in programs with a low degree of recursion, over 90 percent of all procedure calls can be eliminated, with little increase in the size of compiled code and a small savings in execution time"; the savings in execution times he reports vary from 5 to 28 percent. Heindel and Purdom [1967] report that writing certain key subroutines in line in SLIP programs resulted in a 40% decrease in run time and a 3% decrease in program space (SLIP is a list-processing language embedded in FORTRAN). This technique is especially useful on systems that have been designed using data abstraction methodologies (with abstract data types) in which most accesses to data are done with a procedure call; if the substitutions are made mechanically, then we have a clean program with rapid execution time. Kernighan and Plauger [1976, pp. 281-282] report that Dennis Ritchie reduced the run time of a macro processor by a factor of about four by rewriting frequently called procedures as macros that were then expanded in line.

Procedure Rule 1 need not always instantiate all procedures into in-line code; as in many tradeoffs, we can often choose a middle between two extremes. For instance, it might be cleanest to design a particular piece of code as one subroutine with five variables called from ten places. We could replace that by ten different in-line instantiations, as one extreme. A more moderate approach might replace the one subroutine with three subroutines that have, say, just two parameters each, with each one much faster than the single subroutine.

It can be claimed that Procedure Rule 1 takes a nicely structured program and unstructures it for the sake of speed; because of this, some people have deduced that efficiency and clean modularity cannot peacefully coexist. Although that deduction might appear valid, quite the opposite is in fact true. An important cost in most programs is the space they require, and a clean module structure usually reduces that space (as we saw in Time-For-Space Rule 2—Interpreters). Recall that monitoring a program usually shows that a small percentage of the code accounts for a large percentage of the run time; at that point we know which are the expensive data structures in the system, and can then modify them. If the accesses to the structures had been spread throughout the system, then there is no way we could have isolated the costly structures. When we finally do collapse the hierarchy, we can do so in an orderly way (often by changing procedures to macros), so the programmers later involved in the project can still see the highly structured code, even though it is compiled into code less clean and more efficient. Thus Procedure Rule 1 need not unstructure the code, although careful documentation is required if the structure is not to be obscured by its implementation.

The next rule for procedures is related to Logic Rule 3 (Reordering Tests); it formalizes Allen Newell's [1981] maxim that "almost always is almost always as good as always".

Procedure Rule 2—Exploit Common Cases: Procedures should be organized to handle all cases correctly and common cases efficiently.

Jalics [1977, p. 137] used this technique in a routine to calculate Julian dates. He observed that 90% of the calls to the routine had the same date as the previous call, so in those cases he returned the previous answer without recomputing it (this can be viewed as a simple kind of caching). We saw a general application of this rule in Space-For-Time Rule 3: caching data allows us to handle all accesses to it correctly and common accesses efficiently. The basic mechanism for implementing Procedure Rule 2 is simple: we have two routines that accomplish the same end. One is slow but handles all cases correctly; the other handles only special cases but does so quickly. The following are a few of the many ways by which we can ensure that the proper procedure will be executed at run time.

1. All calls in the body of the program are to a new procedure that checks the input and applies the special procedure when it is appropriate and uses the general procedure in other cases. This approach localizes knowledge of the two procedures in the new procedure, but incurs an added cost at run time.

2. Calls in the body of the program are to the special procedure if we can deduce at compile time that it is appropriate; otherwise they are to the general procedure. This saves run time, but compromises program modularity by spreading knowledge of the special procedure throughout the entire program.

3. An intermediate approach has all calls refer to the procedure through a compile-time macro; if that macro can determine at compile time that the special procedure can be called then it does so, otherwise it calls the general procedure. This approach has the advantages of both the above schemes: maximal efficiency is achieved, and knowledge about the special procedure is still localized (in the macro).

The first approach is the easiest to implement in most languages and achieves most of the time savings possible, the third approach can squeeze out a little more time, and the second approach should almost never be used (because it pays too much in maintainability to buy too little in time).

Mary Shaw [1981] used this rule to increase the speed of the system software on the Rice University Computer in 1964. The operating system provided routines to SAVE and UNSAVE registers according to a passed bit string—the routines would store and fetch only those registers whose bits were on. This was an expensive operation (the SAVE routine executed approximately 60 instructions) and was frequently used because the coding style on the machine used short routines and many subroutine calls. Shaw observed that almost all calls to SAVE and UNSAVE (she recalls the number to be upwards of 95%) operated on all registers, so her modified routines tested for that special case and treated it with very efficient code. She also used loop unrolling (Loop Rule 4) and careful exploitation of the assembly language to make the general case faster. These changes reduced the overall run time of some programs by as much as thirty percent.[5]

An important application of Procedure Rule 2 is to observe when a particular subroutine is being used in a certain way, and then to remove from it
unneeded generality. For instance, it might be natural to write a subroutine to
access the Ith element of a sequence of elements, and then ask sequentially for
the first, second, third, up to the Nth elements. For most representations of sequences (including linked lists, trees, and usually even arrays), it would be
preferable to make a new procedure to access the next element. A different approach would use Space-For-Time Rule 3 and cache the address of the most
recently accessed element in the hope that the next element will be near it; this
approach retains state in a procedure across calls. (For a general discussion of
retaining state across calls, see Scherlis [1980, p. 5].) Chris Van Wyk [1981]
found that after modifying the storage allocation scheme of his IDEAL
interpreter as described in Section 3.3, it spent the vast majority of its time in a
general routine for intersecting line segments. Replacing the general (and
simple) routine by a specialized (but more subtle) routine sped up the entire
program by a factor of three on complex pictures. This application of Procedure
Rule 2 is often appropriate when dealing with input and output; it would encourage us, for instance, to have operating system primitives that read or write
entire records instead of forcing the user to access each byte individually through
an operating system call. There are two benefits of this strategy: we can avoid
the cost of many procedure calls and avoid recomputing state across those calls.

A corollary of Procedure Rule 2 is that we should organize systems so that
the efficient cases are common. Rob Pike [1981] used this idea in the design of
a raster-based graphics terminal. Analysis of a preliminary design showed that a
time bottleneck in the overall system was likely to be the BITBLT operation (for
BIT BLock Transfer), which moves a long string of bits from one position in
memory to another. Because the memory was addressable at the bit level but
was actually implemented in 16-bit words, a BITBLT was very expensive if the
source and destination fields did not have the same starting position in the 16-bit
words (aligned moves were four times the speed of unaligned moves). Knowing
that the most expensive use of BITBLT was to move the large portions of the
screen image off the current screen to an invisible part of the memory,

---

[5]Shaw's experience also provides an example of the power of program monitoring. She was
led to the above modification during a discussion with a user about the value of displaying the
program counter on the console lights during program execution. The user did not see the merit in
this, so he and Shaw observed the lights during the execution of one of his time-consuming
programs. When they did so, they found that much of the time was spent in the operating system,
and inspection of the commonly executed code revealed that the only operating system primitives he
used were SAVE and UNSAVE. Patching his code to exploit the special case of operating on all
registers immediately reduced his program's run time by thirty percent. If Shaw could achieve such
speedups in 1964 by staring at the console lights, just think of the speedups that can be achieved
using more sophisticated monitoring tools!

Pike noticed that in that case one could always choose an aligned destination field. This observation reduced the time to save or restore an entire screen from the unacceptably long 0.4 seconds to 0.2 seconds. The speedup was a factor of two rather than a factor of four because the memory could no longer keep up with the inner loop; Pike changed a compute-bound task to be input-output bound.

Procedure Rule 2 encourages us to reduce time by developing specialized procedures; sometimes, though, we can reduce time by developing more general procedures. This fact is so startling that Polya [1945, p. 121] refers to it as the "Inventor's Paradox" and states it as "the more general problem may be easier to solve". Experienced programmers can usually recall seeing the paradox in many circumstances; for instance, it is often more effective in terms of coding effort, run time, and code space to have one procedure for searching tables in a program rather than to have a separate procedure for each table in the program. By having only one procedure we can devote a great deal of energy to making it fast; the payoff of that work is then realized each time the single procedure is called. Furthermore, by looking at a problem in a general setting we often see it more clearly than when it is smothered in detail; that clarity can lead to simpler and faster code. A similar example of using the inventor's paradox to achieve efficiency is when we use an efficient general-purpose system sort routine rather than write a custom sort for each new application. The inventor's paradox has long been realized as an important tool for maintaining correct and maintainable code; we should not let Procedure Rule 2 make us forget that the inventor's paradox can also help us make efficient code.

The next procedure rule can reduce the overhead cost of input and output in many applications.

Procedure Rule 3—Coroutines: A multiple-pass algorithm can often be turned into a single-pass algorithm by use of coroutines.

This technique has been discussed in detail by Knuth [1968, pp. 194-196]. He observes that if program A reads file 1 and writes file 2 sequentially, and is then followed by program B which reads file 2 sequentially and writes file 3, then we can avoid any use of file 2 by keeping both programs A and B in core and allowing them to communicate as coroutines. This is usually faster than the sequential version (because we reduced the costly input/output operations), but requires more space for both data and code. Programs are often easier to design if we think of them as multiple-pass algorithms and then implement them later as single-pass algorithms. Jackson [1975, Chapter 8] discusses this idea as a program design principle he calls "program inversion". The Unix® operating system has made coroutines a fundamental concept in the form of its *pipes* and *filters* (see Ritchie and Thompson [1978, Sections 5.2 and 6.2]).

Recursive procedures (that is, procedures that can call themselves) are powerful expressive tools that can greatly ease the design and implementation of a correct program. That lesson was made clear to me when I translated a

nineteen-step iterative algorithm that I had written (which resulted in over 100
lines of code and took two twelve-hour days to debug) into a four-step recursive
algorithm (which took less than 30 lines of code and took less than an hour to
implement). Unfortunately, this expressive power is not without cost, because
many implementations of recursion are slow. For this reason, a great deal of
work has been devoted to transformations that increase the speed of recursive
programs; see, for instance, Auslander and Strong [1978], Burstall and
Darlington [1976], Bird [1980], Darlington and Burstall [1977], Knuth [1974],
and Standish, Harriman, Kibler and Neighbors [1976]. Because that literature is
so extensive, we will consider here only a few transformations on recursive
procedures, and those only briefly.

Procedure Rule 4—Transformations on Recursive Procedures: The run
time of recursive procedures can often be reduced by applying the following transformations:

- Code the recursion explicitly by use of a program stack. This can
  sometimes reduce costs induced by the system structure, but is often
  slower than using the system procedure calls.[6]

- If the final action of a procedure P is to call itself recursively,
  replace that call by a `goto` to its first statement; this is usually
  known as removing tail recursion. That `goto` can often be transformed into a loop. Knuth [1974, p. 281] and Steele [1977a] both
  contain detailed discussions of this rule.

- If a procedure contains only one recursive call on itself, then it is not
  necessary to store the return address on the stack; see Knuth [1974,
  pp. 281-282]. It is necessary, though, to keep track of the call depth
  in some other way.

- It is often more efficient to solve small subproblems by use of an
  auxiliary procedure, rather than by recurring down to problems of
  size zero or one. This technique was used by Sedgewick [1978] to
  reduce the time Quicksort used in sorting small subfiles and by
  Friedman, Bentley and Finkel [1977, pp. 220-221] to reduce the
  search time of a data structure by a factor of almost two. (This is an
  application of Procedure Rule 2—Exploit Common Cases.)

This list only scratches the surface of techniques for increasing the efficiency of
recursive programs; programmers who use recursion often should read the literature mentioned above.

The final procedure rule we will study is the most system-dependent.

---

[6]Guy Steele [1981] comments that "in general, if the programmer can simulate a construct
faster than the compiler can implement the construct itself, then the compiler writer has blown it
badly".

Procedure Rule 5—Parallelism: A program should be structured to exploit as much of the parallelism as possible in the underlying hardware.

This rule is of course important when we design a program to be executed on a multiprocessor architecture, but it usually surfaces whenever we scrutinize a computing system. For instance, in Expression Rule 5 (Exploit Word Parallelism) we will see that we can exploit the width of a computer word to perform several operations at once. Clever compilers often use the fact that operations set condition codes as a side effect to avoid redundant tests (see, for instance, Russell [1978]); this exploits parallelism at a microscopic level. Many architectures provide "block move" operations that allow us to move many adjacent words in a single instruction (for instance, the IBM System/360-370 has "Load Multiple", "Store Multiple", and "Move Character" instructions). Parallelism is usually present in the operation of the CPU and input/output devices; in some systems one can move work from the CPU to the channels or device controllers (for instance, by using CCW programs in the IBM System/360-370 family). Very high performance computers such as the IBM System/360 Model 91 and the CDC 7600 have many functional units in the central processor that operate in parallel; knowledge about their detailed characteristics can allow us to use that parallelism more efficiently.

These techniques for exploiting parallelism usually are hard to apply and are peculiar to the architecture of the computer on which the program is executed; one should therefore be reluctant to use them. Occasionally, however, they can be used to increase the speed of a program dramatically. Kulsrud, Sedgewick, Smith, and Szymanski [1978] provide a fascinating example of the exploitation of a highly parallel architecture; they describe an implementation of Quicksort on a CRAY-1 that can sort 800,000 elements in less than 1.5 seconds. They employ many general techniques for efficiency (including proper algorithm and data structure selection and careful assembly coding), many techniques of writing efficient code (including loop unrolling, caching the recursion stack, and special treatment of small subfiles), and many techniques specific to highly parallel machines (including chaining operations, careful instruction buffering, and overlapping the execution of independent activities).

5.4 EXPRESSION RULES

In this final section on code modifications we will study techniques that reduce the time devoted to evaluating expressions. Many of these techniques are applied by even relatively simple compilers, so we must be careful that our attempts to help them produce more efficient code do not actually make the object code slower.

The first expression rule that we will see is an extension of Loop Rule 1 (Code Motion Out of Loops). That rule told us to move computation out of a loop, performing a given computation only once rather than many times. The following expression rule treats the many executions of a program as though they were a loop.

Expression Rule 1—Compile-Time Initialization: As many variables as possible should be initialized before program execution.

One application of this rule is usually called "constant propagation"; if we have the statement

```
const X=3; Y=5;
```

in a Pascal program, then the compiler could replace an instance of X*Y later in the program by the constant 15 (some compilers do, some don't). As a more substantial application of this rule, we can return to Fragment K3, which classified characters by using a large table. Peterson [1980] initializes such a table in his program by a procedure that contains four do statements and five assignment statements; initializing the table at compile time would result in a slight increase in the speed of the program and less code. On some systems, though, this change could result in a slight increase in the program's run time, due to reading a longer executable file when the program is loaded.

This application is typical of a larger class of applications of Expression Rule 1. Many programs spend much time reading in data that is unchanged between runs and processing it into tables that are then used for the particular run. Much of that processing and reading time can often be avoided by building a new program that processes the input data into an intermediate file that can then be read and processed more quickly. John Laird [1981] used this technique in a program that spent 120 seconds processing data that was unchanged from run to run, and then less than three seconds processing the data for the given run. A new program processed the unchanged data into an intermediate file (represented in the packed form we studied in Time-For-Space Rule 1) in 120 seconds; his primary program could then read that intermediate file in less than a second. Thus the time required by his program dropped from over 120 seconds to less than four, for a speedup of over a factor of thirty.

The next expression rule arose in a slightly altered form as Logic Rule 1.

Expression Rule 2—Exploit Algebraic Identities: If the evaluation of an expression is costly, replace it by an algebraically equivalent expression that is cheaper to evaluate.

For instance, it would often be more efficient to replace the expression "ln(A)+ln(B)" (where ln is the subroutine for computing natural logarithms) by the algebraically equivalent expression "ln(A*B)". This replacement is inappropriate in some circumstances because many of the properties of real arithmetic do not hold for digital computer arithmetic, and, consequently, laws of algebra often do not apply. Simple applications of Expression Rule 2 are easy to mechanize, and many compilers do quite well at this. (Some FORTRAN compilers, for instance, will observe that if the two terms SIN(X)**2 and COS(X)**2 are added together in an expression, then they can be replaced at compile time by the constant 1!) With this rule, just as with Logic Rule 1, we must avoid "optimizations" that lead to slower code from our compilers.

Steve Johnson [1981] described an algebraic identity that has long been used by compiler writers on two's-complement computer architectures. The problem of testing whether the integer X is between A and B, inclusive (where A<B), arises in implementing both array bounds checking and numeric case statements (such as the FORTRAN computed goto or the C switch). To perform this range check we logically compare X−A with the precomputed value of B−A; the former is greater than the latter if and only if X is not in the proper range. (Logical comparison compares the bit string representation of integers, so that we have the sequence

$$0 < 1 < 2 < \ldots < 2^{L-1} - 1 < -2^{L-1} < \ldots < -2 < -1,$$

where L is the word length of the machine.) The subtraction and comparison needed to accomplish this check are usually faster than the two comparisons required by the straightforward range test, and the common case in which A is zero can be implemented even more efficiently.

Expression Rule 2 can be used when special cases of an expression can be evaluated in a more efficient way than by applying the general rule. For instance, instead of evaluating X**2 by a general routine for raising powers, we can simply multiply X by itself (note that this transformation might also be achieved by Procedure Rule 1—Collapsing Procedure Hierarchies). Similarly, on binary machines we can efficiently multiply or divide by powers of two by shifting left or right (as long as the number is in the proper range; see Steele [1977b]). Knuth [1973, p. 408] used this identity to reduce the MIX run time of a binary search program from $\sim 26 \log_2 N$ to $\sim 18 \log_2 N$.

An algebraic identity is quite useful in increasing the speed of loops. Consider, for instance, the loop "for I := 1 to N do ...", and suppose that we evaluated the expression I*J inside the loop (where J is an integer). The straightforward way of implementing this requires a multiplication in each iteration of the loop, while a more clever implementation can keep the last value of the expression and just add J to get the next. This operation is an instance of a technique called *strength reduction* and is intimately related to techniques for manipulating *induction variables*. For a general discussion of these techniques, see Aho and Ullman [1977, Section 12.2].

Strength reduction is one form of a general technique that Bob Sproull [1981b] refers to as "incremental algorithms". When one deals with a complicated data structure in a loop, that structure can often be updated by making small changes to an existing structure rather than by rebuilding the complete structure from scratch. Note that this method is similar to Loop Rule 1 (Code Motion Out of Loops): we move the code to build the entire structure out of the loop and replace it by code to update the structure. Paige [1979] has given a precise formulation of this method in the high-level SETL language and refers to it as "the formal differentiation of algorithms".

David Jefferson [1981] used an incremental algorithm to decrease the input/output costs of a program simulating interacting organisms on a rectangular grid. The program displayed a series of snapshots describing the locations of the organisms at various time intervals on a character-based terminal. Jefferson observed that the primary time bottleneck of the program was sending the snapshots to the terminal through the serial link; he also noticed that there was typically little difference between successive snapshots. He therefore modified the program to send to the terminal only the changes to the current snapshot, and not the entirety of the new snapshot. This change reduced the number of characters sent to the terminal by a factor of over five for most simulations.

Expression Rule 3 helps us avoid redundant work in evaluating expressions.

> **Expression Rule 3—Common Subexpression Elimination:** If the same expression is evaluated twice with none of its variables altered between evaluations, then the second evaluation can be avoided by storing the result of the first and using that in place of the second.

This is the rule we used to achieve the (unexpectedly small) time savings as we transformed Fragment A1 to Fragment A2. This rule can be viewed as an application of Space-For-Time Rule 2, where we are now storing recomputed results rather than precomputed results.[7] In applying this rule we must be careful not to eliminate expressions whose evaluations have side effects. There are horror stories of sloppy optimizing compilers that would replace the expression Random + Random (where Random returns a random number between zero and one) by the expression 2*Random; although the latter expression is indeed cheaper to evaluate, it does not return the desired result. Many compilers are good at recognizing and exploiting common subexpressions (see, for instance, Aho and Ullman [1977, Sections 14.2 and 15.6] or Wulf et al [1975]), and this technique is often best left to the compiler.

The next expression rule is similar to Loop Rule 6 (Loop Fusion), which encouraged us to let similar loops share their overhead of loop control.

> **Expression Rule 4—Pairing Computation:** If two similar expressions are frequently evaluated together, then we should make a new procedure that evaluates them as a pair.

The hope of this rule is that "two can live as cheaply as one". Knuth [1971, p. 116] observes that while sine and cosine each require 110 time units to

---

[7]Two rules that we have seen previously can be viewed as instances of Common Subexpression Elimination. Loop Rule 1 (Code Motion Out of Loops) eliminates (by motion out) an expression that appears only once in the source text but is common to many iterations of the loop. Expression Rule 1 (Compile-Time Initialization) eliminates evaluation of expressions common to many invocations of a program.

evaluate (where a time unit is approximately .7 microseconds on an IBM System/360 Model 67), a routine that returns both the sine and the cosine of a value requires only 165 time units. We therefore get the second trigonometric function for just half price, after we have purchased the first. A similar phenomenon occurs in finding the minimum and maximum elements of an N-element set; while either alone requires $N-1$ comparisons to find, both together can be found in at most $3N/2$ comparisons (see Knuth [1973, Exercise 5.3.3-25]). This rule is similar in spirit to Procedure Rules 1 and 2—in both cases we reorganize the division of the computation into procedures.

The final expression rule speeds up a program by using the parallelism inherent in the word width of the underlying machine; it is therefore related to Procedure Rule 5 (Parallelism).

Expression Rule 5—Exploit Word Parallelism: Use the full word width of the underlying computer architecture to evaluate expensive expressions.

This rule is used in the implementation of set operations as bit strings; when we or two 32-bit sets together giving as output their 32-bit union, we are performing 32 operations in parallel. Reingold, Nievergelt, and Deo [1977, Section 1.1] describe several algorithms for counting the number of one bits in a computer word (recall that we saw an application of this as we studied Space-For-Time Rule 2—Store Precomputed Results). The first algorithm they describe takes B operations in a B-bit word, an intermediate algorithm takes little space and approximately $\log_2 B$ operations, and an extreme algorithm uses table lookup to solve the problem in constant time, but with 2^B words of space. Beeler, Gosper and Schroeppel [1972] describe similar algorithms for a host of problems on computer words; see especially Items 167, 169, and 175. Weinberger's "quick test" using 32-bit vectors to represent words (described in Logic Rule 3) also exploits word parallelism. All of these techniques have the same motivation as Procedure Rule 5: there is parallelism inherent in the word widths of the underlying data paths and registers, and the algorithms go out of their way to make sure that none of it is wasted in any critical operation.

5.5 EXERCISES

5.1. Write efficient program fragments for the following tasks. Start with simple, straightforward code, and modify it to be as efficient as possible. Your estimate of the efficiency may vary from a count of the high-level language constructs used in the inner loops to measured times of implementations.

   a. Perform a sequential search in a sorted linked list.

   b. Find the minimum element in the N-element vector X[1..N]; assume that all permutations of values are equally likely.

   c. Find the maximum and the minimum elements in the N-element vector X[1..N].

   d. Merge together two sorted sequences to form a third sorted sequence (assume that the sorted sequences are stored in arrays).

e. Search for a given element in a binary search tree; if it is not already in the tree, insert it.

f. Perform an insertion sort in a singly-linked list.

g. Traverse a binary tree (which is not a search tree) to compute the sum of the values in the leaves. Assume that every node in the tree is marked as either a leaf or an internal node; a leaf contains a value, and an internal node contains pointers to its two sons.

h. Reverse a singly-linked list. That is, modify the link fields and the pointer to the first node so that the last element is first, and so on. (This is usually referred to as a destructive list reversal.)

i. [E. M. McCreight] Given the singly-linked list L, return the two lists M and N, where M contains the first Length(L) div 3 elements of L, and N contains the remainder. For instance, if L is the list (A, B, C, D, E, F, G, H), then M is (A, B) while N is (C, D, E, F, G, H).

j. [D. E. Knuth] Given a string of 100,000 characters, count the number of vowels and consonants. (A vowel is an A, E, I, O, or U, and a consonant is any other letter; note that many characters are not letters.)

k. Determine whether the string X[1..100000] of characters contains the pattern Y[1..5]; assume that both strings represent typical English text.

l. Multiply two 512-by-512 boolean matrices giving a third 512-by-512 boolean matrix. Assume that all matrices are stored in a packed format on a 32-bit machine in row-major order, and that you can perform word-parallel boolean operations on 32-bit vectors.

m. The *Move-To-Front* heuristic for sequential search in a sorted array says that whenever the search finds the element X[I], that element should be placed in position X[1] and the old values of X[1..I−1] should all be moved one place to the right. Write a search program that implements this heuristic. (If the value for which the program is searching is not in the array, the program should insert it as the first element.)

n. Turn on all bits from L to U in a 64-bit word, and turn off every other bit. Assume that your language supports the word-parallel boolean operations and, or, xor, not, and versions of the shift operator.

o. Implement Conway's Game of Life (see Gardner [1970] for a description of the game).

p. Implement Prim's algorithm for constructing minimal spanning trees of planar point sets. (See Horowitz and Sahni [1978, Section 4.6] for a description of the algorithm.)

q. Give a function to determine whether the integer N in the range 2..10000 is prime. The routine must be correct for all inputs, and as fast as possible assuming that N is chosen uniformly from the domain. Give two programs: one that is reasonably space-efficient (say, less than a few hundred words of code and data on most machines), and one that uses as much space as possible to achieve blinding speed.

5.2. Show how boolean operators can be used to accomplish the following tasks on 64-bit words without using extra storage.

a. Set every bit in the word A to zero.

b. Swap the contents of words A and B.

5.3. [R. F. Sproull] The purpose of the following routine is to copy CopyCount bytes from an input buffer into an output buffer; the global variable FetchPtr points to the last word copied out of the buffer.

```
for I : = 1 to CopyCount do
    begin
    FetchPtr : = FetchPtr + 1;
    if FetchPtr > MaxBuffer then
        begin
        FillInputBuffer;
        FetchPtr : = 1
        end;
    OutBuffer[I] : = InBuffer[FetchPtr]
    end
```

Show how the two tests in the above inner loop can be reduced to one.

5.4. The benefits of using Procedure Rule 1 vary greatly with the cost of a procedure call; if a procedure call is cheap then the rule gives little speedup, while if a call is expensive then the speedup can be dramatic. Measure the costs of a procedure call on your system, and compare those costs to the costs of simple operations.

5.5. [E. M. McCreight] If linear probing is used to resolve collisions in a hash table, the inner loop in the routine might look like the following.

```
        Start : = Hash(Input);
        I : = Start;
Loop:   if X[I] = Input then goto Found;
        if X[I] = Empty then goto NotThere;
        I : = I + 1;
        if I > TableSize then I : = 1;
        if I = Start then goto Full;
        goto Loop;
Found:      ...
NotThere: ...
Full:       ...
```

Reduce the four tests in the above inner loop to as few as you can, and remove the unconditional branch at the end of the loop. (It is often unwise in practice to push much work out of this inner loop, though, because it is executed few times on the average if the function Hash is effective. This exercise might therefore be an example of premature optimization.)

5.6. Suppose that a program must merge eight sorted files of one-million bytes each into a single sorted file of eight-million bytes. The program currently calls a subroutine to merge a pair of files a total of seven times: it first merges Files 1 and 2 giving the new file M, then merges File 3 with M, then merges File 4 with M, and so on. Give two faster versions of the program.

a. Use the same merge subroutine, but choose a different order in which to merge the files (you may use more than one temporary file).

b. Write a new merge routine.

To analyze each program, give the number of bytes each reads and writes.

5.7. [H. Reisel and D. E. Knuth] In Logic Rule 3 we saw several examples of reordering tests to decrease run time; the purpose of this exercise is to give those examples a precise mathematical basis. Suppose that a program must test for one of N conditions and that condition i costs T_i to evaluate and is true with probability p_i (independent of the other outcomes); in which order should the tests be made?

5.8. [D. A. Moon] Investigate the details of David Moon's PDP-8 interpreter sketched in Logic Rule 4 (Precompute Logical Functions).

5.9. Several of the rules in this chapter can backfire—their application can increase rather than decrease the run times of some programs. Quantitatively analyze this aspect of the following rules: Loop Rule 1 (Code Motion out of Loops), Loop Rule 2 (Combining Tests), Logic Rule 2 (Short-circuiting Monotone Functions), and Logic Rule 4 (Precompute Logical Functions).

5.10. Suppose that a compiler has four phases: lexical analysis, parsing, code generation, and optimization. Discuss the advantages and disadvantages of implementing the phases as separate passes over various files and as a set of coroutines. (For a general discussion of structuring compilers, see Aho and Ullman [1977, Section 1.3].)

5.11. The modifications to code fragments that we have seen in this chapter frequently resulted in longer code that we might suspect is more subtle. One measure of the subtlety of code is the length of its proof of correctness. For this exercise you are to give precise specifications for one of the code fragments in this chapter, verify that the first fragment meets the specifications, and then verify that the later (modified) fragments meet the same (or slightly modified) specifications. What do the lengths of the respective proofs say about the effect of the transformations on the understandability of the code?

5.12. Knuth [1971] describes a statistical study of a set of FORTRAN programs, and gives details on a number of static (compile-time) and dynamic (run-time) properties of the programs; the first part of this problem is for you to study that paper. The second part of this problem is for you to sketch how you would use the statistics in that paper to apply Procedure Rule 2 (Exploit Common Cases) to the task of building a compiler for the FORTRAN language. Consider the efficiency both of the object code that the compiler generates and of the translation from the FORTRAN source code into the object code.

6

SYSTEM-DEPENDENT
EFFICIENCY

In previous chapters we applied efficiency rules in a high-level language with an intuitive understanding of their effect on the resulting system. The guesses were usually accurate: simple rules of thumb describe most of the examples we have seen so far. In this chapter we will study systems that cannot be described by such rules. As an analogy, simple rules usually tell us accurately how distances on a map correspond to driving times in a region, but they sometimes fail. The topics of this chapter are the bumpy dirt roads and the superhighways of computer systems.

The peculiarities that we will study arise from three primary sources: the high-level source language in which we program, the compilation of that program to object code, and the underlying hardware on which the program is executed. In Section 6.1 we will study examples of surprising performance characteristics that arise from those three levels, then in Section 6.2 we will consider some general principles underlying the examples. The reader should be warned at this point that the purpose of this chapter is more to raise questions than to answer them (the answers are, of course, too system-dependent).

6.1 EXAMPLES OF SYSTEM-DEPENDENT EFFICIENCY

In this section we will study a number of small experiments that illustrate the importance of system-dependent efficiency. We will start by investigating several timings of program fragments compiled under the Hamburg Pascal compiler and executed on a Digital Equipment Corporation PDP-KL10 computer.

This compiler produces straightforward object code typical of a large class of non-optimizing compilers. The time anomalies that we will investigate should not be construed as criticisms of the compiler: the compiler performs its intended job well, but the designers chose ease of construction, speed of compilation and reliability over speed of object code. After studying efficiency on this rather simple system, we will investigate efficiency on more complex systems.

6.1.1 Computation Costs on a Simple System

The first pair of Pascal fragments that we will consider both assign the value one to the first N elements in the array X of reals. The first program to do this is the following:

```
for I := 1 to N do X[I] := 1
```

The second fragment is similar.

```
for I := 1 to N do X[I] := 1.0
```

Both programs are correct, but the first fragment required $\sim 48.4N$ microseconds to do the job, while the second fragment required just $\sim 5.4N$ microseconds. The entire difference (an order of magnitude) is accounted for by the ".0" after the "1" in the second fragment. In the first fragment, the "1" is an integer, and every time it is assigned to an element of X, a run-time routine is called that converts the integer to a real (floating-point) number. In the second fragment, the string "1.0" is a real and the assignment proceeds without conversion. An optimizing compiler would probably produce code with the same run time for both fragments: the conversion to real could have been done at compile time (Expression Rule 1) or the code to do the conversion could have been moved out of the loop (Loop Rule 1). This example is typical of many issues of system-dependent efficiency: a two-character modification increases the speed of the program by an order of magnitude, but the naive programmer[1] would never have expected the difference.

The next set of experiments was motivated by Bill Wulf's [1981] comments about the Pascal programs of Chapter 2. He suggested the following system-dependent improvements to Fragment A8:

On almost all machines that I know, counting down to zero is faster than counting up to anything, and a test at the end of the loop is better than a

---

[1] I feel obligated to include myself in that class. I first noticed the cost of run-time conversion when working on the next program fragments in this section and all of the times came out an order of magnitude greater than I thought they would. I found after about half an hour of (frustrating) searching that I had declared the type Pair to contain two reals and then assigned integers to them; the speed difference was entirely accounted for by the conversion to real.

test at the beginning.[2] Thus I don't think that you need to go from Fragment A8 to Fragment A9; rather, you can use the following code.

```
I := HighPt;
repeat
  <Your code from Fragment A8>
  I := I-1
until I=0
```

Also, the fact that `IntArr` is a vector of records implies a more expensive non-unity stride in the array subscript computation. Changing from an array of records to a set of separate arrays is almost always a win. (Remember, you're down to the nitty-gritty at the end here!)

To separate the effect of Wulf's changes from the other intricacies of Fragment A8, Wulf's changes were tested on the following code (which is structurally similar to Fragment A8).

```
type Pair = record A, B: integer end;
var X: array [1..MaxN] of Pair;
begin
for I := 1 to N do
  begin
  X[I].A := I;
  X[I].B := I
  end
end
```

The run time of this code is approximately $15.7N$ microseconds on the Hamburg Pascal compiler.

The first changes to the above fragment tested the various ways of addressing the pairs of integers. The first modification used the Pascal `with` statement[3]; the body of the `for` loop was then

```
with P[I] do begin A := I; B := I end
```

The running time of the fragment dropped from $15.7N$ microseconds to $12.1N$

---

[2]Wulf's second suggestion is exactly the unconditional branch removal of Loop Rule 5. His first suggestion is also of general applicability: it is often advantageous to restructure a tight loop to "count down to zero" to facilitate a more rapid termination test (see Knuth [1968, p. 148, Note 10]). Many computer architectures provide single instructions that implement counting loops; for instance, the IBM System/360-370 has the BXLE instruction (for "branch on index less or equal") and the PDP-11 and VAX have the SOB instruction (for "subtract one and branch").

[3]The `with` statement specifies that the components A and B (which are not associated with particular records by the "." operator) should be associated with the record P[I]. The compiler loads the address of P[I] into a register, so accessing components of the record is particularly efficient.

microseconds. Following Wulf's suggestion of replacing the array of two-component records with two separate arrays reduced the time of the fragment to $10.7N$ microseconds.

The second set of changes took the two-array implementation of the above fragment (that required $10.7N$ microseconds) and modified the for loop by Wulf's first suggestion. The first modification implemented the for loop by a while statement that counted up from 1 to N; that required $12.7N$ microseconds. The second modification implemented the for loop by a repeat...until statement that counted down from N to zero; that required $12.2N$ microseconds. Thus Wulf's suggested structure was indeed faster than the corresponding while statement, but was slower than the for statement supplied by the compiler.[4] (We saw a similar phenomenon in Fragment E2 in Loop Rule 2.)

The examples of this section can be summarized in the following point:

- In high-level languages functionally equivalent programs can have different costs; the programmer should therefore know the costs of various constructs and use the cheapest for the system at hand when writing system-dependent efficient code.

6.1.2 Computation Costs on Complex Systems

Our view of system-dependent efficiency in the previous section was on a relatively straightforward system: the Hamburg Pascal compiler on a PDP-KL10. We will now briefly consider two more subtle systems: the C language under the Bell Telephone Laboratories compiler on a PDP-11 and the Bliss language under the Bliss-11 compiler described by Wulf *et al* [1975] on a PDP-11. Both systems share the subtleties of the PDP-11 architecture (see Wulf *et al* [1975] for a simple description of the machine), but their other complexities come from different sources. In the next program we will study, the key to an efficient inner loop is the use of automatic incrementing and decrementing during the execution of a PDP-11 instruction. Both programs that we will study eventually achieve this, but for different reasons.

- The C language supports the construct x[i + +] that returns the value of the ith element of x and has the side effect of increasing the value of i. Likewise x[i--] returns x[i] and post-decrements i. The constructs x[+ +i] and x[--i] are similar, but they perform the operations on i

---

[4]It is interesting to observe the code the Hamburg compiler generates for the various loop-control constructs. The for loop generates a loop with four control instructions in the main loop (a for loop that counts down with the downto option uses the same number). The while loop has four loop control instructions and three instructions for adding one to I; the repeat loop has only three loop control instructions. The one instruction that the repeat loop is missing is the goto at the end of the loop (using Loop Rule 5).

before accessing the ith element (that is, the i$+$1st or i$-$1st element is returned).   The C language also allows explicit declarations that certain variables be kept in registers and permits arithmetic operations on pointers (in particular, one can increment the pointer p by the operation p$++$). The C compiler does relatively little optimization; it consists only of an optional phase after the rest of the compilation and performs only local changes.   Thus programmers achieve efficiency in C by expressing the appropriate constructs in the source language.

- The Bliss language is a more typical Algol-class language, but the Bliss compiler performs a number of optimizations.   Efficiency in Bliss is gained by the programmer expressing a source-level language program that does not present any obstacles to optimization; after that, the compiler takes care of the rest.   The Bliss language also allows the programmer to control the low-level primitives, but these are not frequently used; because so many optimizations are performed by the compiler, the typical use of Bliss is more like the use of other Algol-class languages.

We will investigate the issue of exploiting the full power of the underlying architecture in a high-level language by examining efficient implementations of Fragment I4 in C and Bliss.   We will first study a sequence of C programs written for a PDP-11/70 by John Majernik of Bell Telephone Laboratories in Columbus, Ohio.   Majernik first transliterated Fragments I1 through I4 to C; we will call those Fragments M1 through M4.   His first fragment (excluding declarations) is shown below.

```
for (i = 2; i <= n; i = i+1) {
    j = i;
    while (j > 1 && x[j] < x[j-1]) {
        swap(&x[j], &x[j-1]);
        j = j-1;
    }
}
```

Fragment M1.   Transliteration of Fragment I1.

This fragment is a faithful transliteration of Fragment I1 from Pascal to C; it is not coded in typical C style.   The second and third fragments were similar to their Pascal counterparts (recall that they involved writing the Swap procedure in line and moving assignments to and from T outside the loop).   The fourth C fragment (which added a sentinel at x[0]) is as follows:

```
x[0] = minusinfinity;
for (i = 2; i <= n; i = i+1) {
    j = i;
    t = x[i];
    while (t < x[j-1]) {
        x[j] = x[j-1];
        j = j-1;
    }
    x[j] = t;
}
```

Fragment M4.   Transliteration of Fragment I4.

The coefficients of the run time of the four fragments were respectively 12.3, 6.9, 4.2, and 3.6 microseconds (that is, the run time of Fragment M1 was $12.3N^2$ microseconds); all programs were compiled with the optimizer turned on.

Majernik's next fragment, M5, was the same as Fragment M4, except that the variables i, j, and t were declared "register int", to tell the compiler to place them in registers. The run time of that program was $2.3N^2$ microseconds, for a speedup of about 35 percent. His next fragment replaced the indices into the array by pointers; the resulting code was as follows:

```
int i;
register int *j;
register int t;
register int *k;

x[0] = minusinfinity;
for (i = 2; i <= n; i++) {
    t = *(j = k = &x[i]);
    while (t < *(--k)) {
        *j-- = *k;
    }
    *j = t;
}
```

Fragment M6.   Final C fragment.

This fragment makes extensive use of C constructs to achieve efficient machine code; operating indirectly through pointers avoids the overhead of array accessing. The inner loop of the machine code has only four instructions and makes only eight memory references; the run time of this fragment is $1.0N^2$ microseconds.

Majernik's experiment is summarized in Table 6.1. That table gives the run time coefficients for the insertion sort Fragments I1 through I4 and Majernik's Fragments M1 through M6. The first row of the table says that Fragment I1 had a run time on the PDP-10 of $6.00N^2$ microseconds, which is 2.97

times the run time of Fragment I4; Fragment M1's PDP-11 run time was $12.3N^2$ microseconds, which is 3.4 times the run time of Fragment M4. The absolute run times in Table 6.1 are inviting comparisons of apples and oranges: the PDP-KL10 is a faster machine than the PDP-11/70, but the program on the former is sorting 36-bit real numbers while the latter is sorting 16-bit integers. For this reason, comparisons should not be made between the absolute times in the table, but only between the normalized times.

Table 6.1. Times of insertion sorts.

Fragment Number	Pascal Fragments		C Fragments	
	Time	Normalized	Time	Normalized
1	6.00	2.97	12.3	3.4
2	3.99	1.93	6.9	1.9
3	2.73	1.35	4.2	1.2
4	2.02	1	3.6	1
5	—	—	2.3	.64
6	—	—	1.0	.28

Table 6.1 tells a convincing tale. The language-independent changes gave a speedup of a factor of 3.0 in Pascal and 3.4 in C; furthermore, the speedups were similar in both languages. The language-dependent changes that Majernik made then gave an additional factor of 3.6, for a total speedup of a factor of over 12.

Bob Chansler of Carnegie-Mellon University and I conducted an experiment similar to Majernik's in which we used the Bliss language and the compiler described by Wulf *et al* [1975]. Fragments I1 through I4 were transliterated to Bliss; the number of instructions in the inner loops of the four fragments was 24, 20, 13, and 12, respectively. (It was not possible to time the programs on a PDP-11/70 like that used by Majernik, but the instruction counts give an accurate idea of the quality of the code.) Chansler then inverted the loop, using the Bliss equivalent of the Pascal repeat...until statement, and changed from array indexing to pointers; this gave an inner loop of three instructions with six memory references (recall that Majernik's best inner loop in C had four instructions and eight memory references). Chansler's code, incorporating a modification suggested by Bill Wulf, was as follows:

```
macro dec(x) = (x=.x-2)$;

global routine sort = begin
local t, j, k;
x[0] = minusinfinity;
incr i from 2 to .n do
   begin
   j = x[2*.i];
   k = .j-2;
   t = ..j;   j = .j+2;
   if .t gtr ..k then do dec(j) = ..k
                          until .t leq .dec(k);
   dec(j) = .t
   end
end;
```

This program is convoluted, but it does yield object code with an inner loop with
one-fourth the number of instructions of the inner loop from the best transliterated fragment.[5]

There are two conclusions we can draw from our investigation of complex
systems.

- The system-independent rules of Chapters 4 and 5 can be effective in complex computing systems. They gave a speedup of a factor of 3.0 in Pascal, 3.4 in C, and 2.0 in Bliss in the example of this section.

- System-dependent efficiency techniques can have a tremendous effect
  beyond that of system-independent rules. In the C example they decreased
  the run time by a factor of 3.6, while in the Bliss example they decreased
  the number of instructions in the inner loop by a factor of four.

6.1.3 Input/Output Costs on a Simple System

The examples of the previous sections dealt only with the costs of performing
computations. That is important in compute-bound systems (on which we have
been concentrating throughout this book), but the dominant cost in many systems
is that of performing input and output. We will now briefly study the costs of
performing input/output on the Hamburg Pascal system described previously.

The first set of tests exercised reading and writing eight-character packed

---

[5]In fairness to the Bliss compiler, it is important to observe that such an extreme increase in
speed is rare. This code exercises heavily operations on arrays, while the Bliss compiler did not
include some well-known array optimizations, such as strength reduction (Expression Rule 2). This
is because Bliss was designed as a systems programming language, and such operations rarely arise
in systems programs. The object code that Bliss produces from straightforward statements of most
tasks is usually close to that produced by experienced hand-coders.

strings, declared as var X: packed array [1..8] of char. For both reading and writing, two separate procedures were used. The first used the built-in Pascal instructions for reading and writing strings (i.e., readln(X) and writeln(X)). The second procedures used for loops to process individual characters; the following is the write procedure:

```
for I := 1 to 8 do
  write(X[I]);
writeln
```

For the read procedures, the costs were respectively 1.5 milliseconds and .93 milliseconds for the built-in read and the for-loop read. For the write procedures, the costs were .27 milliseconds for the built-in write and .69 milliseconds for the for loop. (All times were determined by timing several executions of procedures that read or wrote 1000 eight-character strings.) For reading strings, the built-in operation was 1.6 times more expensive than using the for loop, while for writing the built-in operation was 2.6 times *cheaper* than the for loop.

The second set of exercises tested reading eight-digit integers in three ways. The first method read each integer by reading into a real number and rounding that to be an integer; that required 2.01 milliseconds. The second method read the integer directly (which required 1.95 milliseconds), while the third method used a for loop to read each character and performed the conversion to integer within the program (that method required just .81 milliseconds). The for loop program was about 2.5 times faster than the other programs.

One must be careful in generalizing from these examples of the Pascal input/output system. There are, however, two that I feel safe in making:

- The costs of performing input/output in various ways can vary widely. We saw examples in which the costs varied by a factor of 2.5; replacing the slow operation by the fast operation in an input/output bound system could drop the system cost to forty percent of what it was.

- One should be hesitant to draw general principles about input/output systems. When we observed that reading strings with built-in operation was 1.6 times slower than using the for loops we might have assumed that a similar relation would hold for writing strings; in fact, we saw that writing with built-ins was 2.6 times *faster* than writing with for loops.

6.1.4 Hardware Issues

The above examples of system-dependent efficiency dealt with the high-level source language, the compilation of that language to machine code, and input/output systems. We will now briefly consider several hardware issues that can have a profound effect on the efficiency of program execution.

- **Instruction Costs.** Different implementations of the same architecture often have different relative costs for the same instructions. For instance, the

IBM System/360 architecture is implemented in several different computers. On the Model 40, the "or immediate" (OI) instruction is 2 times faster than an "add normalized short" (AE) instruction. On the Model 75H, the AE instruction is 1.9 times faster than the OI instruction. (Both of these ratios were derived from IBM functional characteristics manuals.) When two different instructions are available for accomplishing the same task, the programmer should know which is more efficient and should be able to employ the more efficient.

• **Register Allocation.** Storing a variable in a register increases a program's efficiency in two ways. The running time is usually decreased because registers are usually realized by a faster technology than main memory and are architecturally (and usually physically) closer to the arithmetic and logical unit. A variable in a register also requires fewer bits to address; this means that the instruction is faster to access and that the overall program will require less space. Guy Steele [1981] reports that on the PDP-10 architecture it is possible to execute extremely tight loops by placing them in the registers, and this was often done on the model KA10 in critical loops. Although it is still possible to execute code from the registers on the (later) model KL10, it is actually slower to do so than executing code stored in main memory.

• **Instruction Caching.** Many high-speed computers have a cache for the recently accessed instructions; if a tight loop fits in that cache then it will run more quickly than if the instructions must be fetched repeatedly from main memory. Dongarra and Hinds [1979] describe an example in which unrolling a loop (by Loop Rule 3) two, three, and four times progressively decreased the loop's running time, while unrolling it a fifth time *increased* its running time. The problem was that unrolling it the fifth time caused the loop to be larger than the instruction cache. This phenomenon occurs often as one unrolls loops in high-performance computers.

• **Storage Layout.** The layout of a program's storage in memory can have a significant effect on the execution speed of the program. Bill Wulf [1981] advises Bliss programmers to ensure that arrays contain records of length that is a power of two; this enables the multiplication of the array index by a left shift (which is often cheaper than multiplication by an arbitrary integer). On the other hand, programmers on the high-performance CRAY-1 computer are advised to declare 64-element vectors to be of length 65 to avoid the memory contention that would occur if all vectors started on the same address (modulo sixteen), because the memory is realized in sixteen modules.

• **Caching.** If an operating system offers a user a larger virtual memory than that allocated on the physical machine, then the larger memory is usually implemented by dividing the virtual memory into pages and keeping only active pages in main memory (the inactive pages are stored on disk).

Knowledge of the interaction of the paging structure and the storage layout can have a profound effect on efficiency. Suppose, for example, that we wish to store a 512-by-512 array on a system that has 512-word pages. In many systems the array would be stored as 512 pages in which each page contained exactly one row of the array. Accessing each element of the array by traversing the array by rows would require 512 disk reads or about ten seconds, assuming a 20-millisecond read. On the other hand, if we traversed the array by columns, then we would have to make more than a quarter of a million disk reads, which would take over an hour and a half.

Jim Gosling [1981] exploited this structure in a BASIC program on a Digital Equipment Corporation PDP-11/45 under the RSX-11M operating system. He was hired as a consultant to reduce the run time of a program to simulate fluid flows through a system of pipes; when he started on the project, the program required three days for a simulation, which was longer than the mean time between failures for the particular machine. Gosling rearranged the matrix structure to interact more gracefully with the caching structure (much like the above example), and thereby reduced the running time of the program to approximately thirty minutes, for a speedup by a factor of approximately 150. McKellar and Coffman [1969] provide a general study of organizing matrices in paged systems.

This list is not meant to be exhaustive, but it does indicate several important sources of system-dependent efficiency (and inefficiency) at the hardware level.

6.2 PRINCIPLES OF SYSTEM-DEPENDENT EFFICIENCY

In the previous section we saw several anecdotes of system-dependent efficiency. In this section we will consider the issue more generally by identifying several sources of system-dependency. We will then study several questions about those sources that can aid a programmer making design decisions about efficiency.

In the transformations of Chapter 2 we made changes to the program that we thought would improve performance and then observed the new program to measure the time difference. It would be more desirable to have an analytic tool that would predict the performance improvement. One such tool has been described by Shaw [1979]; she gives a set of measurements of the clock times that various Pascal instructions require (on the same compiler and machine used in the experiment of Chapter 2). Table 6.2 shows Shaw's costs for the various Pascal operations; that table is excerpted from Figure 6.3 of Wulf, Shaw, Hilfinger and Flon [1981, p. 165].[6]

---

[6]WULF, W. A., M. SHAW, P. N. HILFINGER, and L. FLON [1981]. *Fundamental Structures of Computer Science*, © 1981 Addison-Wesley, Reading, MA. Reprinted with permission.

Table 6.2. Costs of Pascal operations.

Operation	Cost (Microseconds)
assignment (:=)	1.1
if statement, then branch	0.8
if statement, else branch	0.8
while loop, terminal test	1.5
while loop, normal iteration	0.8
for loop, terminal test	2.0
for loop, normal iteration	1.8
parameterless function call	5.6
value parameter	1.3
var parameter	1.1
test relations (>, >=, =, <>)	0.5
integer +	0.5
integer −	0.7
integer *	2.5
real +	2.0
real -	2.3
real *	2.8
simple variable fetch	0.1
single subscript calculation	2.2

An experiment was conducted to compare the empirically observed run times of the programs in Chapter 2 with the analytic estimates given by Shaw's method. The cost of each Pascal operation was determined from Table 6.2, with the exception of the sqrt function, which was assumed to have a cost of 42.8 microseconds. The results of the experiment are shown in Table 6.3; the first row of that table says that Shaw's method estimated that Fragment A2 would require $43.05N^2$ microseconds, while it was observed to require $45.6N^2$ microseconds. The final column shows that Shaw's estimates were close to the observed times. Having these performance statistics for a particular compiler/machine pair allows us to fine-tune our code for that system with a little analysis replacing a lot of measurement.

Table 6.3. Analytic predictions of times.

Program #	Empirical Time	Analytic Time	Analytic/ Empirical
2	45.6	43.05	0.944
3	24.2	21.65	0.895
4	21.2	18.85	0.889
5	14.0	12.9	0.921
6	8.2	7.05	0.860
7	7.5	6.1	0.813
8	6.8	5.0	0.735

Table 6.3 shows that simple cost models for compiler/machine pairs can be accurate in predicting the run times of programs; such a cost model would be helpful for a programmer tuning code to run on a particular system. Shaw's model can serve as a prototype for a simple model for other systems. To be even more useful, her model could be extended to include costs of operations that are not indicated textually. For instance, we saw earlier that assigning an integer value to a real variable on the Hamburg Pascal system invokes a run-time routine that requires 40 microseconds (while a real multiplication costs only 2.8 microseconds); that cost is not accounted for in Shaw's model. Likewise, a more useful cost model would describe the expense of various input and output operations.

Leverett [1977] provides an excellent introduction to the issues of evaluating the computational performance of high-level language systems. He studies two main classes of evaluation techniques: comparative evaluations run benchmark programs on several different systems (see, for instance, Wichman [1976]), and analytic evaluations study the structure of a single system. He surveys the results of many evaluation experiments, and then presents his own detailed study of the performance of an Algol-68 system on a PDP-11. Anyone interested in developing a system like Shaw's for a particular compiler should certainly read Leverett's paper.

Although a simple model such as Shaw's can work well for a simple compiler (such as the Hamburg Pascal compiler), it is more difficult to describe the efficiency of code produced by highly optimizing compilers. Such compilers perform so many optimizations that the object code often bears little resemblance to the source code. At first inspection, it might appear that the only way to know which of two high-level language programs is faster is to compile both and then either run them or inspect the object code. For some programs this is true, even for programmers familiar with the particular optimizing compiler.

We will now investigate a technique that can often give us insight into whether a proposed change would increase a program's efficiency (but it will not tell the exact cost of a code fragment). Many of the optimizations in Chapters

4 and 5 are performed by optimizing compilers; these include Loop Rules 1, 5 and 6 (Code Motion Out of Loops, Unconditional Branch Removal, and Loop Fusion), Logic Rule 1 (Algebraic Identities), Procedure Rule 1 (Collapsing Procedure Hierarchies—specifically, writing procedures in line), and Expression Rules 1, 2 and 3 (Compile-Time Initialization, Algebraic Identities—specifically, strength reduction, and Common Subexpression Elimination). We should learn which optimizations are performed by the compiler we are using, and then never use those and always use the others when improving critical program fragments. This leaves us with the problem of determining which optimizations our compiler employs, but it is usually easy to find simple (approximate) models of what the compiler does. For instance, to determine whether a compiler moves code out of loops (Loop Rule 1), we can time the executions of Fragments C1 and C2, and observe the time differences. Likewise, we can test many of the other optimizations with simple programs (usually less than a dozen lines long). Such simple tests can often tell us which optimizations are useless and which are priceless under a particular compiler.

The problems of predicting performance and of writing system-dependent efficient code become more important for interpreted (rather than compiled) systems. Because many actions are performed at run time (such as statement retrieval, statement parsing, and variable-name binding), simple textual style can have a profound effect on program run time. For instance, Gunther [1981] asserts that the performance of BASIC programs can be improved by techniques such as putting frequently accessed variables at the front of declaration lists, placing frequently used code at the start of the program, writing multiple statements on a single line, and eliminating comments. All those modifications can be explained by a simple model of the run-time actions of the interpreter, and each can help to reduce the number of expensive run-time actions.

The introduction to this chapter promised only to raise questions about system-dependent efficiency, and not to answer them. The examples of Section 6.1 show why this is: many issues are so related to particular systems that no general principles can be drawn. This section, though, shows that even if we cannot have a set of general answers, we can at least have a set of general questions. Thus before we attempt to make a particular program efficient on a given system, we should have (at least rough) answers to the following questions.

- **The High-Level Language.** What are the relative costs of the various constructs in the language? What are the cheapest possible ways to accomplish common operations (i.e., input and output, or iterating through the elements of a vector)?

- **The Compiler.** What optimizations does the compiler perform, and what optimizations should the programmer perform? Which language constructs encourage the compiler to perform optimizations, and which constructs block optimizations?

- **The Machine Architecture.** Which efficient operations in the underlying hardware are easy to access, and how can the compiler give access to them? Is there an instruction buffering scheme that makes certain instruction organizations more efficient than others? What paging or caching schemes does the machine support, and how can the program's locality structure be organized to exploit the schemes?

6.3 EXERCISES

6.1. Take a particular program that has been tuned to be efficient across a variety of systems, and further tune it to be efficient on a particular system. You should consider at least two kinds of programs.

    a. **Compute-Bound Programs.** Consider any of the programs in Chapters 2, 4 and 5.

    b. **Input/Output-Bound Programs.** Any input/output-bound program will do; see, for instance, most of the programs described by Kernighan and Plauger [1976]. Counting the number of words in an input file usually results in an input-bound program; copying an input file to an output file exercises both input and output.

6.2. Perform tests on your particular system to determine the following:

    a. The costs of primitive operation; prepare a table like Table 6.2, but more extensive.

    b. The costs of input/output operations.

    c. The kinds of optimizations performed by the compiler.

6.3. Write a short (say, twenty-page) handbook for your system that tells programmers how to achieve system-dependent efficiency when they need it. Try to address all of the issues mentioned in this chapter that are relevant to your systems. (Part of your handbook should include the measurements of Exercise 6.2.)

7

APPLYING THE TECHNIQUES

In previous chapters we have seen a number of tools for writing efficient code. In Section 7.2 we will review the rules of Chapters 4 and 5 and consider their application as a collection. Before we do that, though, in Section 7.1 we will consider three fundamental rules that underlie any application of the other rules.

7.1 FUNDAMENTAL RULES

All of the rules in Chapters 4 and 5 assume that the code to which they are applied defines a simple (but perhaps expensive) computation. If the code is needlessly complex, then we should apply the following rule from Kernighan and Plauger [1978, p. 131].

> **Fundamental Rule 1—Code Simplification:** Most fast programs are simple. Therefore, keep code simple to make it faster.

There are two primary sources of harmful complexity: a lack of understanding of the task and premature optimization (which we saw already is the root of most programming evil). Both of these distractions should be removed before we attempt to apply efficiency rules; we must understand the essence of the program and then express it in its simplest form. It is common to find that the simpler program is more efficient than the complex version (see, for instance, Kernighan and Plauger [1978, pp. 131-133]).

What the above rule does to the code that solves the problem, the next rule does to the problem itself.

Fundamental Rule 2—Problem Simplification: To increase the efficiency of a program, simplify the problem it solves.

Many of the rules in Chapters 4 and 5 reflect this principle. For instance, Loop Rule 1 (Code Motion Out of Loops) simplifies the task of a loop by doing extra work outside the loop, and Logic Rule 4 (Precompute Logical Functions) reduces the hard problem of computing a logical function to the simple problem of table lookup.

A more dramatic application of this rule salvaged a data-entry program in BASIC on a personal computer system. The system was designed to handle a maximum record length of 250 digits, while typical records were of length 80. In the first implementation of the program I dealt throughout with 250-digit records. When the operator hit the "ENTER" key, the system took approximately five seconds to pack the first record; to pack the last record stored in internal memory required forty-five seconds (the increase was due to the added overhead of garbage collection). When the system was reorganized to process and store only the digits actually used, the time to process each record was less than a second. Simplifying the problem to be solved from storing all possible digits to storing only the active digits required changing only two lines of code (due to system support of variable-length records) and made an unbearably slow system quite comfortable.

The next fundamental rule describes the attitude the programmer should have once he has identified the critical parts of the expensive system.

Fundamental Rule 3—Relentless Suspicion: Question the necessity of each instruction in a time-critical piece of code and each field in a space-critical data structure.

Knuth [1974, p. 267] describes this attitude as follows: "I now look with an extremely jaundiced eye at every operation in a critical inner loop, seeking to modify my program and data structure ... so that some of the operations can be eliminated". We have seen before that this rule can be harmful when applied too early. When applied properly, though, it is the master key to writing efficient code: the techniques of previous chapters remove certain inefficiencies, but the mind set of this rule suspects inefficiency in every critical line of code and often finds it. The programmer who has taken this rule to heart longs to turn his sluggish system into a "lean, mean computing machine" and therefore trims every unneeded cycle from the inner loops and every unneeded bit from the large data structures.

The final Fundamental Rule is not new in this chapter, but rather provides a uniform view of a number of rules that we have seen previously.

Fundamental Rule 4—Early Binding: Move work forward in time. Specifically, do work now just once in hope of avoiding doing it many times later.

Previous rules we have seen in this book can be viewed as instances of this meta-rule[1]. Space-For-Time Rule 2 (Store Precomputed Results) and Logic Rule 4 (Precompute Logical Functions) are obvious applications of this rule. Loop Rule 1 (Code Motion Out Of Loops), Expression Rule 1 (Compile-Time Initialization), and Expression Rule 3 (Common Subexpression Elimination) all move code from places where it is executed many times to places where it is executed just once. Procedure Rules 1 and 2 (Collapsing Procedure Hierarchies and Exploit Common Cases) involve doing extra work at compile time to avoid work at run time; in the former rule the work identifies the sequence of calls to be made, and in the latter rule the work recognizes the common case.

I had an opportunity to use this rule in the design of a program that was to be run on a personal computer about a dozen times per day. In the first (clean) implementation I was surprised to find that an apparently innocuous procedure called just once per run required fourteen hours of processing time on typical inputs, while the rest of the program required just forty-five minutes. By applying techniques described in this book to two expensive three-line loops in that procedure, I was able to reduce its time to two hours and twenty minutes. Although that reduction was easy to achieve, additional speedups would have been quite difficult. The purpose of the procedure was to compile a file into a table that was then selectively processed by later parts of the program. Monitoring the use of the program showed that each file was typically built into a table three times. I therefore added routines and operator commands to store and retrieve the finished table on disk; thus each table was (expensively) built just once and then was (cheaply) read from a disk file whenever it was subsequently needed. The total speedup of the procedure was a factor of eighteen: a factor of six by tuning was augmented by a factor of three by system reorganization to exploit early binding.

An important application of this meta-rule replaces work done by the computer during program execution with work done by the programmer during program development. For instance, many systems perform subscript-checking to ensure that array indices are within bounds; Knuth [1974, p. 269] discusses how the programmer can show correctness analytically as the program is being developed, and therefore safely turn off expensive run-time checking. In Time-For-Space Rule 1 (Packing) we saw that careful analysis of a program's space could allow us to overlay two logical data structures in one array. There are many similar applications of this rule: they all trade programmer thought for computer cycles. Given the relative costs of the two kinds of processors, that tradeoff is usually unwise to make, but sometimes it can be cost-effective.

It is interesting to compare Fundamental Rule 3 with Space-For-Time Rule

3 (Lazy Evaluation). Both rules deal with programs that contain an expensive function that is defined on a certain domain, which we will call D, and is evaluated for every element of a set E. If the function is evaluated at each element of E only once, then we should evaluate the element as it is needed. On the other hand, if many elements of E are evaluated often, then we should store the values by one of the following two schemes, rather than recompute them.

- If the set E contains almost all of the elements of the domain D, then we should use a straightforward application of Space-For-Time Rule 1 (Store Precomputed Results) and store the values of the function on every element in D.
- If the set E is much smaller than D, then we should use Space-For-Time Rule 3 (Lazy Evaluation), and evaluate and store the elements of E only as they are needed.

7.2 APPLYING THE RULES

The most important point about efficiency was made in Section 3.1: we should almost never consider efficiency in the first design of a module, and rarely make changes for efficiency's sake that convert clean, slow code to messy, fast code. Knuth's [1971] statistics quantify this: he observed (and many have since verified) that in most compute-bound programs about four percent of the code usually accounts for fifty percent of the run time. We saw in Section 3.1 that this fact helps us to concentrate our search for efficiency on that critical four percent; we will now consider two deeper implications that the statistics have for efficiency improvements to systems.

- If our goal in increasing the efficiency of the system is to increase the speed as much as possible in a short period of time, then we should monitor the program to find the hot spots and focus our work on them. Using a number of efficiency techniques often enables us to decrease the time of many of the critical regions by up to an order of magnitude. If we achieve such a speedup, then we will have increased the efficiency of our system by a factor of about two (because the remaining 96 percent of the code accounted for about half of the original run time).
- If our goal is to increase the efficiency of our entire system by a factor of twenty, then it will be very difficult to accomplish. The first step is the one described above: we identify the initial hot spots and reduce those; this might reduce the total system time by a factor of two. We then instrument the resulting program, and try to reduce the time spent by the new resource sinks, and iterate. The hope of this strategy is that the system will have a jagged time profile at each iteration; that is, we hope that no matter how many improvements we have made, that most of the run time is still concentrated in a small percentage of the code. Unfortunately, it is the ex-

perience of most programmers that after a few rounds of optimizations, system profiles become flat, and dramatic time improvements are then harder to achieve.

These points put efforts on efficiency in perspective: they are often useful to reduce dramatically the run time of a costly piece of code (say, by an order of magnitude or more). Several such changes can have a tremendous effect on the speed of an entire system (say, up to a factor of ten), but it is difficult to have more impact than that without working at many design levels.

After we have identified the crucial operations in the system, we should bring to bear the efficiency tools at the most amenable of the design levels discussed in Section 1.2. For some systems, we can change the overall system structure, or modify the underlying system software and hardware (many of the techniques in Chapters 4 and 5 are also applicable to the design of efficient hardware; see McFarland [1981]). For most programmers, though, the primary efficiency change they should consider is to modify the intramodular structures by changing their underlying data structures and algorithms. Sometimes, however, even the best algorithms and data structures give programs that still require too much time. The techniques of Chapters 4 and 5 make local changes to programs that can dramatically reduce the run times of critical modules. The methodology of Section 3.3 implies that those techniques should only be used when the following conditions are satisfied.

- The programmer has made certain that efficiency is an important problem in the given system (in particular, it is usually unwise to invest a lot of programmer time in a program that is executed infrequently).
- The particular piece of code being modified is a major bottleneck in the overall system performance.
- All the major speedups achievable by replacing the underlying algorithms and data structures have been incorporated.

Once the hot spots of a system have been isolated, there are four critical steps in applying the rules of Chapters 4 and 5.

1. **Identify the code to be changed.** We should identify the code to be changed by monitoring the program, and then concentrate on the parts that are taking the majority of the time.

2. **Choose a rule and apply it.** Once we know what code to change, we see if any of our rules can be used to change it. The rules have been presented in groups as they relate to different parts of programs; we should therefore identify whether the expense of our program is going to data structures, loops, logic, procedures or expressions, and then search in the appropriate list for a candidate rule. When we apply a rule, we should make sure that the application preserves the correctness of the program; this is usually done by applying the spirit, if not the actual formulas, of program verification.

3. **Measure the effect of the modification.** The first transformation we saw in Chapter 2 (removing the common subexpression from Fragment A1) was typical of many changes we make: it appeared that it would increase the program's speed by a factor of two but in fact it gave less than a three percent improvement. Even if we believe that we understand the effect of a transformation by reasoning alone, it is absolutely necessary to support that analysis with observation; we often find that we are quite mistaken.

4. **Document the resulting program.** The final modified program should include a description of the clean code and of the modification that was incorporated for efficiency.[2] That description can range from a brief comment to including a copy of the original code enclosed within comment characters and a thorough discussion of the rule used to modify it (with an appropriate reference to this book, of course).

Each of these four steps plays a crucial role in yielding a correct and efficient program, and none of them should be skipped in applying the rules. The rules themselves are summarized in Table 7.1 (a more detailed summary of the rules can be found in Appendix C); we will now briefly discuss each class of rules as a set.

---

[2]This suggestion dates from the antiquity of computer science; McCracken [1957] addressed the issue as follows.

[S]uppose a coding trick is used in performing some function of the program. Tricks save time and/or storage space, and one usually derives a certain pleasure from writing a clever program. However, a tricky program is difficult to read after the details are forgotten. A note in an assertion box makes the trick clear.

Table 7.1. Summary of the rules.

Modifying Data Structures

Trading Space-For-Time	*Trading Time-For-Space*
1. Data structure augmentation	1. Packing
2. Store precomputed results	2. Interpreters
3. Caching	
4. Lazy evaluation	

Modifying Code

Loops	*Logic*
1. Code motion out of loops	1. Exploit algebraic identities
2. Combining tests	2. Short-circuiting monotone functions
3. Loop unrolling	3. Reordering tests
4. Transfer-driven loop unrolling	4. Precompute logical functions
5. Unconditional branch removal	5. Boolean variable elimination
6. Loop fusion	

Procedures	*Expressions*
1. Collapsing procedure hierarchies	1. Compile-time initialization
2. Exploit common cases	2. Exploit algebraic identities
3. Coroutines	3. Common subexpression elimination
4. Transformations on recursive procedures	4. Pairing computations
5. Parallelism	5. Exploit word parallelism

If monitoring the program shows that a certain data structure is a primary user of a scarce resource, then we should use the rules of Chapter 4 to make that structure more efficient. At the time we modify the structure we should know whether space or time is dearest, and then trade the cheaper commodity for the more expensive. Although each rule was expressed in terms of trading one resource for the other, by reversing each we can make the trade in the opposite direction.

If we find that the primary resource bottleneck is time spent in a loop (as we often do), then we should apply the loop rules of Section 5.1 to remove every piece of excess baggage from the loop. Although each of the six loop rules typically reduces the run time by between ten and thirty percent, when they are carefully applied together to a single loop it is not uncommon to see speedups of factors of three or more.

The logic rules of Section 5.2 should be brought to bear when the time spent in evaluating program state is in the system bottleneck. Logic Rules 1 and 5 sometimes shave a small percentage from the system run time, but sometimes fool compilers into producing slower object code. Logic Rules 2 and 3 are applicable less often, but can sometimes cut in half the time required by code. Logic Rule 4 is perhaps the most powerful of all: we can frequently eliminate most of the time spent in evaluating a logical function simply by precomputing all possible outcomes.

The procedure rules of Section 5.3 make the most global of the changes that we have seen. Procedure Rules 1 and 2 are the most frequently applied and often yield substantial speedups. Procedure Rules 3 and 4 are powerful in certain special cases (if we have a multiple-pass or recursive program). Procedure Rule 5 is the most nitty-gritty: if we know a great deal about the parallelism in the underlying hardware, then we can exploit it.

The expression rules of Section 5.4 in their purest senses should usually be brought to bear only as a last resort. They are often done by a compiler, they are perhaps the easiest to apply incorrectly, they rarely yield enormous speedups, and their application can result in slower object code. Occasionally, though, they can be used to shave ten percent here or twenty percent there. Many of those rules, though, can be used in a more global sense than that in which they are usually considered. When most people speak of compile-time initialization, they refer to computing certain values at compilation. We saw in Section 5.4 that the same technique can be used to reorganize an entire system so that expensive computations are performed only once. Several of the other rules can be generalized to large systems, with substantial reductions in the time consumed by the resulting programs.

There are two important caveats for all of the rules. The first is that their application can introduce bugs into a correct program; for this reason each rule must be meticulously applied and the resulting program should be thoroughly tested. The second caveat is that every rule can backfire, and actually decrease the efficiency of the program. (For instance, moving code out of loops by Loop Rule 1 decreases efficiency if the loop is never executed.) For this reason, it is absolutely necessary to time each program after it is modified.

Programmers will sometimes find themselves able to apply two or more of the rules to a given problem. While it is often the case that two rules are totally independent (that is, both can be applied to the program without interfering with each others' jobs), in some contexts applying a given rule could either block the application of a second rule or open the way for the application of a third. When a programmer has several options open, two simple heuristics can help him decide which rule he should use first. The first heuristic is to use the *greedy* approach of making the change that yields the greatest improvement; this can be misleading, but usually gives good results. The second heuristic is that the programmer should always be willing to *backtrack* and undo a previous change if that is necessary to implement a potentially more profitable change. Steve Johnson [1981] once found that undoing a change that had a year previously given a big speedup resulted in a new speedup; other optimizations and changes in usage patterns meant that what had been a speedup was now a slowdown.

The programmer applying these rules for the first time should be careful not to overuse them. The first few applications of the rules often have a substantial impact on the running time of the system, without doing much harm to the program's maintainability. Later changes usually have less impact on the running time (because the first changes concentrated on the most obvious hot spots), and they lead to a program that is progressively more difficult to maintain (as more code becomes more subtle). We saw an example of this in Chapter 2: Fragment A6 was good enough for the two applications described in that chapter, and the next three transformations dirtied the code substantially without much increase in efficiency. Although the exact location of the point of diminishing returns for the rules is learned only from experience, programmers should be aware that such a point does exist.

If system-independent techniques fail to yield an efficient system,[3] then one should bring to bear system-dependent techniques such as those discussed in Chapter 6. Although these techniques can improve performance substantially, the program will usually not maintain its efficiency as it is transported to other host systems. If the resulting system is still too inefficient, then one should consider implementing the expensive operations in assembly code or even in microcode.

7.3 EXERCISES

7.1. There is only one possible exercise for this chapter: increase the efficiency of a large program. Choose a program, if possible, that is currently consuming large amounts of resources. As you work, take measurements that will allow you to give quantitative answers to the following questions.

　　a. Did the run-time profile initially display obvious peaks? How did the profile change after several rounds of optimization?

　　b. What design levels facilitated the greatest speedups? What was the relative importance of changing data structures, changing algorithms, and writing efficient code? Were you able to work at any other design levels?

　　c. Did the nature of the modifications change as more modifications were made? Did later modifications give less of a speedup? Did they require longer to make? Did they require more lines of code? Did you reach a point of diminishing returns for improving efficiency?

---

[3]Sometimes system-dependent techniques should be brought to bear earlier: Waldbaum [1978] reports that his group was able to increase the performance of several expensive programs simply by increasing the optimization level under which they were compiled. This kind of system-dependent optimization is well worth its price and should almost always be incorporated before a program is put into production.

8

SORTING AND SEARCHING

In Chapters 4 and 5 we studied a set of efficiency rules and applied them to small code fragments, and in Chapter 7 we considered applying the rules in large software systems. In this chapter we will take an intermediate view by studying two programming problems of fundamental importance and several programs to solve each efficiently. Writing efficient code will be a major tool in our quest for efficiency, but we will also broaden our scope to employ tools at other design levels. We will especially consider improvements at the design level of changing the intramodular structure. To this end, the problems of this section employ useful algorithms; as such, this chapter is designed to be a miniature introduction to the study of algorithms.

8.1 SORTING

In this section we will briefly study one of the central problems in computer science: sorting a table of elements. This problem is important for a number of reasons. It arises in many programs; students in a first programming course often need to write a simple sort routine to solve their problems. The subject has great mathematical depth: Knuth [1973, Chapter 5] devotes over 480 pages to sorting, and mentions hundreds of open problems. Another reason that sorting is interesting is its great practical importance: Knuth [1973, p. 3] reports that computer manufacturers estimated that "over 25 percent of the running time on their computers is currently being spent on sorting". Sorting is a fundamental, deep and important problem.

To study this general problem we will consider only the following special instance of the sorting problem.

Write a) program to sort an array of 1000 real numbers stored in primary memory into nondecreasing order. Specifically, we are to permute the elements of the vector $\overline{X[1..N]}$ so that that they satisfy the relation

$$X[1] \leq X[2] \leq \ldots \leq X[N].$$

Furthermore, we cannot assume that the input vector X is usually given in any particular order. This problem is to be solved one thousand times per day, so speed is crucial.

Sorting becomes a different problem for much smaller and much larger sets, for sorting (say) long strings rather than reals, and for sorting sets stored on external media; throughout the rest of this section, we will ignore those possibilities. We will also assume that we have established that this is the *right* problem to solve and that this sorting problem is indeed in the program's time bottleneck. We will therefore be justified in devoting a great deal of time in this section to making an effective program to solve this particular sorting problem.

Whenever I have to write a sort routine (which happens frequently), my first response is to use Fragment I1, the insertion sort that we studied at the end of Section 5.1. That program is short (only five lines of code, excluding lines that contain only begin or end), easy to understand, well-tested, and correct. If efficiency is not a concern, this is usually the right procedure to use. In this problem, though, efficiency is crucial. The $6.0N^2$ microsecond running time of this program means that it will take six seconds to solve the 1000-element problem; solving the problem one thousand times requires an hour and forty minutes. One approach to a more efficient program for this sorting problem is to fine-tune Fragment I1; we did exactly this at the end of Section 5.1. That effort resulted in Fragment I4, whose running time of $2.0N^2$ microseconds solves this problem in two seconds (and solves the problem one thousand times in about thirty-three minutes). We could increase the performance of this method even further by employing the system-dependent techniques of Chapter 6 or even hand-coding an assembly language program to exploit the full efficiency of the underlying machine. If we were really lucky, this approach might yield up to an order of magnitude increase in performance, but it will be hard to get more than that by working at these design levels.

Our course of action should now be to work at a different design level; the most fruitful approach appears to be to change the structure of the sort module by using a new sorting algorithm. Once we decide to do this, we should refer to Knuth's [1973, Chapter 5] definitive work on sorting algorithms. That approach makes this exercise a little *too* easy, though, because Knuth has written a superlative treatise on sorting. We will therefore pursue a course we could take for a wider variety of problems, and study the topic of sorting in a general algorithms text. In particular, we will refer to the excellent text by Aho, Hopcroft, and Ullman [1974].

Chapter 3 of that text is devoted to sorting. On page 93 the authors describe an algorithm due to C. A. R. Hoare named `Quicksort` and state that its running time is "a fraction of other known algorithms when implemented on most real machines". Since this is exactly what we want to do, this sounds like the algorithm we should explore.

`Quicksort` is based on the algorithm design principle of "divide-and-conquer": it solves a problem by breaking it into small subproblems and solving those recursively. Aho, Hopcroft, and Ullman [1974, p. 94] give the following high-level description of the `Quicksort` algorithm.[1]

```
procedure Quicksort(S);
if S contains at most one element then return S
else
   begin
      choose an element V randomly from S;
      let S₁, S₂ and S₃ be the sequences of
          elements in S less than, equal to,
          and greater than V, respectively;
      return (Quicksort(S₁) followed by S₂ followed
              by Quicksort(S₃))
   end
```

It is easy to see that this program is correct: if the elements are correctly divided into the subsets S_1, S_2 and S_3, then the entire routine will be correct. Analysis of the algorithm shows that it makes approximately $\sim 1.4N \log_2 N$ comparisons.

The text then goes on to consider two details that arise in implementing the algorithm as a program. The first concerns the selection of the partitioning element, $\dot{V}$: the authors advise that the program should select a random element of its input as V. The second detail is the representation of the sets and the implementation of the partitioning into sequences S_1, S_2, and S_3. At this point it is easiest to let the authors speak for themselves; the following is from Aho, Hopcroft, and Ullman [1974, pp. 95-97], with slight changes for consistency with the notation of this section.

> As `Quicksort` calls itself recursively, its argument S will always be in consecutive array entries, say $X[L]$, $X[L+1]$, ..., $X[U]$ for some $1 \leqslant L \leqslant U \leqslant N$. Having selected the "random" element V, we can arrange to partition S in place. That is, we can move S_1 to $X[L]$, $X[L+1]$, ..., $X[K]$, and the union of S_2 and S_3 to $X[K+1]$, $X[K+2]$, ..., $X[U]$ for some K, $L \leqslant K \leqslant U$. Then, S_2 and S_3 can be split up if desired, but it is usually more efficient to simply call `Quicksort` recursively on S_1 and the union of S_2 and S_3, unless one of those sets is empty.

[1]AHO, A. V., J. E. HOPCROFT, and J. D. ULLMAN [1974]. *The Design and Analysis of Computer Algorithms*, © 1974 Addison-Wesley, Reading, MA. Reprinted with permission.

Perhaps the easiest way to partition S in place is to use two pointers to the array, I and J. Initially, I = L, and at all times, X[L] through X[I−1] will contain elements of S_1. Similarly, J = U initially, and at all times X[J + 1] through X[U] will hold elements of the union of S_2 and S_3. The routine in Figure 3.8 will perform the partition. [That routine is given in Fragment N1 under the comment "Partition around V".]

After the partition, we can call Quicksort on the array X[L] through X[I−1], which is S_1, and on the array X[J + 1] through X[U], which is the union of S_2 and S_3. However, if I = L, in which case S_1 is empty, we must first remove at least one instance of V from the union of S_2 and S_3. It is convenient to remove the element on which we partitioned. It should also be noted that if this array representation is used for sequences, we can pass arguments to Quicksort simply by passing pointers to the first and last location of the portion of the array being used.

With that description in hand, it is fairly easy to implement a Quicksort program, which results in the code shown in Fragment N1.[2]

---

[2]There was a bug in Figure 3.8 in the first printing of Aho, Hopcroft, and Ullman's text: the first while statement tests i < j but should test i <= j. That bug is fixed in later editions.

```
procedure Quicksort(L, U: ArrPtr);
  var I, J: ArrPtr;
    V: real;
  begin
  if U > L then
    begin
    (* Place the random element V in X[U] *)
    I := L+trunc((U−L+1)*Random);
    Swap(X[I],X[U]);

    (* Partition around V *)
    V := X[U];
    I := L;
    J := U;
    while I <= J do
      begin
      while (X[J] >= V) and (J>=L) do J := J−1;
      while (X[I] <  V) and (I<=U) do I := I+1;
      if I < J then
        begin
        Swap(X[I],X[J]);
        I := I+1;
        J := J−1
        end
      end;

    (* Special case of all elements > V *)
    if I=L then
      begin
      Swap(X[L],X[U]);
      I := I+1;
      J := J+1
      end;

    (* Recursively sort subarrays *)
    Quicksort(L, I−1);
    Quicksort(J+1, U)
    end
  end;
```

Fragment N1.   Initial implementation of `Quicksort`.

The type ArrPtr is defined to be an index into the array X, and Random returns a random number uniformly distributed between zero and one. The procedure is used to sort the entire array by the call Quicksort(1,N); its average running time on a 1000-element array under the Hamburg Pascal compiler is 0.40 seconds. Using this program one thousand times requires about seven minutes.

Fragment N1's running time of 0.40 seconds is a factor of five faster than the 2.0 seconds of Fragment I4; we will now increase the performance of Quicksort even further by using the efficiency rules of Chapters 4 and 5. Before we do so, we should use monitoring tools to identify the expensive parts of Fragment N1. Such tools would tell the same story that Aho, Hopcroft, and Ullman derive by a mathematical analysis: most of the operations of the procedure are performed in the partitioning phase. We should therefore concentrate our attention on the loop that begins while I <= J. As soon as we identify that code as the inner loop, the call to the Swap procedure stands out like a sore thumb: it is a procedure call in an inner loop. We should therefore rewrite the innermost if statement as in the following fragment.

```
if I < J then
  begin
    T:=X[I]; X[I]:=X[J]; X[J]:=T;
    I := I+1;
    J := J-1
  end
```

Fragment N2.   Rewrite swap procedure in line.

The above fragment has an average running time of 0.38 seconds on vectors of size 1000, which is a five percent improvement.

The next part of the inner loop to which our attention is drawn is the two while statements. Both of those loops have short bodies and complicated tests, so we should try to apply Loop Rule 2 (Combining Tests). The purpose of the loop is the comparison of V to an element of X, while the other test is just bookkeeping. We can remove the second test by ensuring that whenever the call Quicksort(L,U) is made, X[L-1] is less than elements of X[L..U] and X[U+1] is greater than all of those elements. To accomplish this we must execute the following statements once before ever calling Quicksort.

```
X[0]   := MinusInfinity;
X[N+1] := PositiveInfinity;
```

(Note that assuming the existence of infinite values and storing outside the array bounds can make this a less than general-purpose sorting routine.) The inner loop of the partitioning phase then becomes the following.

```
while I <= J do
  begin
  while X[J] >= V do J := J-1;
  while X[I] <  V do I := I+1;
  if I < J then
    begin
    T:=X[I]; X[I]:=X[J]; X[J]:=T;
    I := I+1;
    J := J-1
    end
  end;
```

Fragment N3.   Remove index tests from inner loops.

The average running time of this program on a 1000-element vector is 0.34 seconds; one thousand sorts require less than six minutes.

So far we have concentrated our attention on the partitioning phase of the program, and the remainder of Fragment N1 has remained unchanged. This is appropriate for large values of N, because analysis shows that statements in the inner loop of the partitioning procedure are executed about $1.4N \log_2 N$ times, while every other statement is executed at most N times. However, in our problem N is 1000 and the inner loop statements are executed only about 14 times more often than other statements, so the other statements can still have a substantial impact on the run time. If we were to run Fragment N3 on a system that profiles how much time was spent in each procedure, then we would find that a large portion of the Quicksort time is spent in calls to the subroutine Random (which requires 120 microseconds; 1000 calls require 0.12 seconds). Thus a large portion of the run time of Fragment N3 is spent in computing random numbers. Further analysis shows that almost all of the calls to Random occur when Quicksort is sorting small files.

This analysis shows that we have a recursive procedure that is efficient for large sets but is slow on small sets. Procedure Rule 4 (Transformations on Recursive Procedures) offers a solution to exactly this problem: we should solve small subproblems not by the general recursive procedure, but rather by an auxiliary procedure. Furthermore, we have just the right tool for the job: the insertion sort of Fragment I4 is efficient for small problems. We can easily modify that procedure to sort the array fragment X[L..U] by changing the outer for loop from "for I := 2 to N" to "for I := L+1 to U". Fragment N4 is a modified Quicksort that sorts files with no more than CutOff+1 elements by insertion sort, while larger files are sorted recursively.

```
procedure Quicksort(L, U: ArrPtr);
  var I, J: ArrPtr;
      T, V: real;
  begin
    if U−L <= CutOff then
        InsertionSort(L,U)
      else
        begin
        *** Code from Fragment N3 body here.
        end
  end;
```

Fragment N4.   Treat small subfiles separately.

The final task in implementing the Quicksort of Fragment N4 is to choose an appropriate value of CutOff. If we had in hand both a complete mathematical analysis of the Quicksort algorithm and accurate costs of each Pascal operation, then we could determine the best value of CutOff by a mathematical analysis (Knuth [1973, Section 5.2.2] uses this approach). Because that method involves more work than most programmers can put into a single program, we will take another approach that involves less mathematical analysis and usually gives the correct answer. Namely, we can measure the program's running time using different values of CutOff, and then choose the best value.[3] Such measurements for Fragment N4 are shown in Table 8.1; the first row of that table says that when CutOff was 1, the average running time of the program to sort a 1000-element vector was 0.265 seconds.

Table 8.1. Run time as a function of CutOff.

Cutoff	Run Time
1	0.265
3	0.197
5	0.167
10	0.134
20	0.123
25	0.117
30	0.116
35	0.126
40	0.129
50	0.137
80	0.163
120	0.220
150	0.249

---

[3]The weakness of this approach is that we might never look in the right range for the optimal value of CutOff, and therefore choose a locally optimal but globally suboptimal value.

The optimal value for `CutOff` appears to be 30, but any value between 10 and 50 leads to overall performance within twenty percent of optimal. Choosing `CutOff` as 30 results in a run time of 0.12 seconds to `Quicksort` a 1000-element array; one thousand such sorts require two minutes.

We now have a reasonably efficient sorting program. Whereas our first program (Fragment I1) requires an hour and forty minutes to sort one thousand 1000-element tables, the final program (Fragment N4) requires just two minutes to do the job. It seems to be hard to squeeze any more time from this program, and the two minutes per day spent on sorting would go unnoticed on most systems, so we have probably reached the point of diminishing returns in reducing the time spent in sorting. (On the other hand, two minutes per day is still one hour per month or half a day per year, so it might be profitable to reduce the time even further.)

Before we leave the sorting problem, there is one important point to emphasize: the `Quicksort` program of Fragment N4 shouldn't be used in most applications. That program was derived by taking the initial Fragment N1 from Aho, Hopcroft, and Ullman [1974], and then improving it by a factor of about 3.3 using rules from Chapter 5. If we needed a `Quicksort` program in an application, we could do better yet by consulting a reference that discusses `Quicksort` implementations in detail, such as Knuth [1973, Section 5.2.2] or Sedgewick [1978]. Implementing Sedgewick's algorithm resulted in a program with a run time of 0.08 seconds, which is about 30% less than the 0.116 seconds of Fragment N4. (Sedgewick achieves the speed by a more sophisticated scheme for choosing V, a simpler partitioning strategy, and use of the more efficient `repeat-until` control structure for the innermost loops in the partitioning phase.) This experience should put the rules in context: they were sufficient to achieve a large part of the speedup between the 0.40 seconds of Fragment N1 and the 0.08 seconds of Sedgewick's program, but the *years* of careful study that Sedgewick devoted to `Quicksort` cannot be replaced by any set of rules.

8.2 SEARCHING

In this section we will study another of the central problems of computer science: searching to determine whether a given element is in a table. Like sorting, searching is important for several reasons: it arises in many programs, it is mathematically deep (Knuth [1973, Chapter 6] devotes 215 pages to the problem), and it is of great practical importance. As with sorting, we will study the huge problem of searching by considering only a small subproblem.

> Write a procedure to search to see whether a given real number is in an array of 1000 real numbers. Specifically, we are to see whether the real number T is contained in the real array X[1..N]; if it is in position I we return I, and if it is not in the array we return 0. A typical application of this subroutine will be *N* searches that search once for each element in the

array X[1..N]. One million searches are performed per day, so speed is crucial. The search procedure is the only procedure to use the array X[1..N], so we have the liberty of spending a small amount of time organizing the array before any of the searches are performed.

The problem of searching once for each element in the array is not interesting in itself. Rather, it is a way of specifying two facts that may be important as we design a program: most searches find what they are looking for, and no elements are searched for with higher frequency than others.

The first program that comes to mind when I have to solve a searching problem is the simple linear search described as Fragment D1 in Section 5.1. It is correct, well-tested, and reasonably efficient. Its search time of ~7.3C microseconds implies that in a table of 1000 elements, it will average 3.65 milliseconds to answer a single query (because C, the number of comparisons it makes, is ~$N/2$ on the average). Performing one million searches will require a little more than one hour. Using a sentinel at the end of the array in Fragment D2 reduces the time of an individual search to ~4.1C microseconds, and one million searches then require a little more than 33 minutes.

There are a number of avenues we could explore to increase the speed of sequential search. We could use the sequential search for sorted tables described in Fragments E1 through E4. Unfortunately, keeping the table sorted increases the speed only of unsuccessful searches (those that do not find the element they are searching for), and our assumption states that unsuccessful searches are rare. A second avenue we could explore is to put the commonly accessed elements near the front of the table, where they would be found soon by the sequential search (this was discussed in Space-For-Time Rule 3—Caching). The assumption also shows that this approach would be to no avail: no elements are searched for with higher frequency than the others.

It seems that to achieve a dramatic speedup we will have to abandon the sequential search and change the structure of the search module. The method that most programmers would now use is binary search. In this approach, we must use our freedom to permute the elements of the array and sort the array into nondecreasing order. Since we are going to perform many searches and sort the array just once, we will probably use the straightforward insertion sort of Fragment I1.

It is easy to describe the binary search algorithm to determine whether T is in the sorted array X[1..N]. The invariant of the algorithm is that at all times we have a range of values (which we denote by L..U) such that if T is anywhere in the array, then it is in X[L..U]. Initially, the range is the complete array. The algorithm proceeds by choosing an element of X from the center of the range and comparing it to T. There are three possible outcomes of the comparison: if T is less than the element then we continue the search with the range truncated above the element (that is, the old value of U becomes one less than the position of the element of X), if T is greater than the element then we continue with the range truncated below the element, and if T is equal to the element then we return the position of the element. This process continues until we either find the element we are looking for or the range of potential values for the element becomes empty. When this algorithm is applied to an N-element table, it makes approximately $\log_2 N$ comparisons both in the worst case and on the average.

With this description of binary search, it seems to be a simple task to implement a binary search program. Unfortunately, many of the subtleties of the programmer's art are needed, and it is remarkably easy to write an incorrect program. Knuth [1973, p. 419] points out that sixteen years passed from the first published description of binary search to the first published program that works correctly for all inputs. In a class I taught to twenty-two professional programmers (most with more than ten years' experience) there was a two-hour assignment to write a binary search program; after inspecting their programs for thirty minutes, eighteen of the programmers found bugs in their code. Because this program is so difficult, we would do well to take a correct binary search program from an established reference; we will again turn to Aho, Hopcroft, and Ullman [1974, Section 4.3]. (As with sorting, our problem would be a little *too* easy if we turned immediately to Knuth's [1973, Chapter 6] treatise on searching.) Fragment O1 is taken almost directly from Figure 4.3 of Aho, Hopcroft, and Ullman; the only changes are in the variable names and the convention used to return the location of T.

```
procedure Binary(T: real; L,U: ArrPtr;
                 var P: ArrPtr);
  begin
  if L>U then
      P := 0
    else
      if T = X[trunc((L+U)/2)] then
          P := trunc((L+U)/2)
        else if T < X[trunc((L+U)/2)] then
          Binary(T, L, trunc((L+U)/2)-1, P)
        else
          Binary(T, trunc((L+U)/2)+1, U, P)
  end;
```

Fragment O1.   Initial implementation of binary search.

To search an N-element table with the above procedure, we make the call

```
Binary(T, 1, N, Position)
```

When the routine returns, Position will contain the position of T in the table if it is there, and otherwise contain zero. The running time of this program to perform a single search in a 1000-element table is 2.56 milliseconds; performing one million searches requires over 42 minutes, which is slower than the sequential search of Fragment D2.

I was shocked when I made the above measurements: the binary search took more time to make ten comparisons than the sequential search did to make five hundred! While each operation in the sequential search required just 4.1 microseconds, each of the $\log_2 N$ steps of the binary search required approximately 256 microseconds. It is clearly time to work on the efficiency of the code in the binary search program. There is one obvious inefficiency in Fragment O1: the expression `trunc((L+U)/2)` is evaluated three times on most invocations of the procedure. We can avoid this by applying Expression Rule 3 (Common Subexpression Elimination) and storing the value of the expression in the variable M (which is the middle of the range we are considering). This results in the code of Fragment O2.

```
begin
M := trunc((L+U)/2);
if T = X[M] then
    P := M
  else if T < X[M] then
    Binary(T, L, M-1, P)
  else
    Binary(T, M+1, U, P)
end
```

Fragment O2.   Store common subexpression in M.

This change reduces the run time to search a 1000-element array from 2.56 milliseconds to 1.01 milliseconds; the time for each of the ten steps of the search dropped from 256 microseconds to 101 microseconds.

These statistics imply that each evaluation of M requires 77 microseconds; since we still have one left, it is consuming the vast majority of the time of the procedure. A moment's thought reveals the origin of the huge time of this apparently simple function: the semantics of Pascal declares that the expression `(L+U)/2` is evaluated as a `real` number; therefore both L and U are converted to `real` numbers, the division is carried out as a `real` division, and the result is then converted back to an `integer` by the `trunc` function. (And recall that the first example in Section 6.1.1 showed that conversion from one internal representation to another can be very expensive.) We can avoid the cost of converting to and from real numbers by using the Pascal operator for integer division, `div`, as in Fragment O3.

```
M := (L+U) div 2;
```

Fragment O3.   Change evaluation of M.

The resulting program requires 230 microseconds to perform a binary search in a 1000-element table; each basic operation now requires only 23 microseconds, rather than the 101 of the previous fragment.[4]

The one remaining expensive operation in Fragment O3 is the recursive procedure call. In general, it is difficult to remove recursion from a procedure, but this procedure happens to have one of the special forms discussed in Procedure Rule 4 (Transformations on Recursive Procedures). Both of the recursive calls in the procedure occur as the last statements in the procedure (this is called tail recursion), so we could in principle replace them by goto statements. An alternative approach is to enclose the entire procedure within a loop-endloop statement, and to break from that loop only when the recursive program would return immediately. Following either approach leads to the program in Fragment O4.

---

[4]Some readers of preliminary drafts have argued that reporting the time reduction of replacing the conversions and real division with an integer division is cheating; they assert that "programmers who know Pascal would have used integer division in the first place". I originally used the other form for two reasons: it was the most faithful translation of Aho, Hopcroft, and Ullman's [1974] procedure, and it is the way I usually perform this operation (I was unaware of its high cost until performing these tests). Those who argue that we should always use integer division are perhaps placing too heavy an emphasis on efficiency too early in the development process.

```
procedure Binary(T: real; IL,IU: ArrPtr;
                 var P: ArrPtr);
var L, U, M: ArrPtr;
begin
L := IL;
U := IU;
loop
  if L>U then
      begin
      P := 0;
      break
      end;
  M := (L+U) div 2;
  if T = X[M] then
      begin
      P := M;
      break
      end
    else if T < X[M] then
      U := M−1
    else
        L := M+1
  endloop
end;
```

Fragment O4.   Convert recursion to iteration.

The input parameters IL and IU are the input to the procedure; the variables L and U are initialized to contain the input parameters. The running time of this procedure on a 1000-element table is 160 microseconds; each of the ten operations costs approximately 16 microseconds (a reduction of about thirty percent from Fragment O3).

Inspection of the inner loop of Fragment O4 reveals only one errant practice: the if statement in that loop tests for the *least* common outcome first. The most common path through the loop for a successful search in a 1000-element table is that T is not found in the first nine iterations and is then found in the tenth. The code as it now stands tests for equality at each of the nine iterations and, not finding it, makes one additional test. We can reduce the average number of tests made in those iterations from two to one-and-a-half by a simple application of Logic Rule 3—Reordering Tests. If we first test whether T is to one side of the middle element, then half the time we are successful and make only that one test; the other half of the time we must make two tests. Fragment O5 shows the if statement that incorporates this change.

```
if T < X[M] then
    U := M-1
  else if T > X[M] then
    L := M+1
  else
    begin
    P := M;
    break
    end
```

Fragment O5.   Order tests.

This procedure requires 150 microseconds to perform a binary search in a table of 1000 real numbers; the cost of each of the $\log_2 N$ operations has been reduced from 16 microseconds to 15 microseconds.

Fragment O5 is about seventeen times faster than Fragment O1; while Fragment O1 requires over 42 minutes to perform one million searches, Fragment O5 requires just two-and-a-half minutes. In most applications, that is fast enough: two-and-a-half minutes per day is a small part of a computing budget. If more speed is required, then there are two obvious improvements that could be easily achieved in assembly language. The first improvement is to replace the div operator by a shift one bit to the right (this is an application of Expression Rule 2—Exploit Algebraic Identities). The second improvement is the implementation of the second comparison of T to X[M]: the Pascal compiler re-evaluates the comparands and then compares them, while on many machines an assembly coder could just retest the condition code (this is an application of Expression Rule 3—Common Subexpression Elimination). These improvements combined with careful assembly coding could probably squeeze another factor of three from the run time of the binary search on most computers (compared, of course, with code produced by simple compilers).

Fragment O5 (with the assembly language modifications described above) is probably close to the best we can do by applying the general techniques of this book to Aho, Hopcroft, and Ullman's original program. If we need more speed, then we should consult Knuth's [1973] definitive treatise on searching. Section 6.2.1 discusses binary search, and Exercise 6.2.1-11 describes an extremely efficient binary search program; Fragment O6 is a Pascal implementation of that program, tailored to searching 1000-element tables.[5]

---

[5]This program has a bug: if T is less than all elements of X[1..N], then the last comparison will access X[0], which is out of bounds. This bug could be fixed by initially assigning I to be one, but that complicates the intuitive explanation of how the procedure works.

```
procedure Binary1000(T: real; var P: ArrPtr);
(* Binary search for T in X[1..1000] *)
var I: ArrPtr;
begin
I := 0;
if X[512] <= T then I := 489;
                          (* 489 = 1000-512 + 1 *)
if X[I+256] <= T then I := I+256;
if X[I+128] <= T then I := I+128;
if X[I+64] <= T then I := I+64;
if X[I+32] <= T then I := I+32;
if X[I+16] <= T then I := I+16;
if X[I+8] <= T then I := I+8;
if X[I+4] <= T then I := I+4;
if X[I+2] <= T then I := I+2;
if X[I+1] <= T then I := I+1;
if X[I] = T then
    P := I
  else
    P := 0
end;
```

Fragment O6.   Knuth's binary search.

The operation of the procedure is easy to understand if we consider what happens when the test $X[512] <= T$ fails. We then know that if T is anywhere in the table, it must be in $X[1..512]$; the next nine comparisons determine the successive bits of T's location in the table if it is there, most significant digit first. The final comparison checks whether or not T is actually in the table. When the test $X[512] <= T$ succeeds, the same kind of search is performed in the 512-element table $X[489..1000]$. The running time of the program is 57 microseconds; the cost of each of the $\log_2 N$ operations is about 5 microseconds. One million searches require about one minute.

Fragment O6 could *in principle* be synthesized by applying the rules of Chapter 5 to Fragment O5. We use Expression Rule 2 (Exploit Algebraic Identities) to change the representation of ranges from lower and upper bounds to a lower bound and a distance. The first comparison in the procedure applies the corollary of Procedure Rule 2 (Exploit Common Cases) that states that we should organize systems so that efficient cases are common; that comparison ensures that the search will always be performed in a 512-element table. Loop Rule 3 (Loop Unrolling) unrolls the loop entirely and writes all of its constants in line. Logic Rule 2 (Exploit Algebraic Identities) and Loop Rule 1 (Code Motion Out of Loops) then postpone the test for equality until after the loop. *In fact*, though, code as efficient (and elegant) as the above can only be achieved by careful study.

It is possible to achieve an even more efficient binary search by working at the lower design level of translation to machine code. The Hamburg Pascal compiler translates each of the nine similar lines in Fragment O6 into eight PDP-10 instructions; during execution, six of those are executed on the average. Guy Steele [1981] transliterated the Pascal program into the Bliss language and compiled it under the Bliss compiler for the PDP-10; that resulted in just two machine instructions for each of the nine similar lines.[6]During execution of the program one of those is always executed while the other is executed half the time, on the average; the average cost of execution of the pair of instructions is approximately .9 microseconds. When Steele carefully hand-coded a binary search (using the inner loop produced by the compiler), the complete time for a binary search in a 1000-element table was just 12.1 microseconds; performing one million searches required 12.1 seconds.

8.3 DISCUSSION OF THE PROGRAMS

In this section we will consider some implications of the previous two sections. To aid us in this endeavor, the work of those sections is summarized in two tables. Table 8.2 describes the sorting algorithms in Section 8.1. The first row of that table says that Fragment I1 has a run time of approximately $6.0N^2$ microseconds to sort N elements; it requires approximately 0.06 seconds to sort 100 elements, 6.0 seconds to sort 1000 elements, and 10.0 minutes to sort 10,000 elements. The run times for the insertion sorts were derived in Section 5.1. The run time formulas for the `Quicksort` programs were not discussed in the text; they were derived by curve-fitting constants to formulas in Knuth [1973, Section 5.2.2] and they accurately describe observed data.

---

[6]The Bliss compiler translated the Bliss equivalent of the Pascal instruction

```
if X[I+256] <= T then I := I+256
```

into the PDP-10 instructions

```
CAML T,X+256.(I)
ADDI I,256.
```

when I is declared to be in a register.

Table 8.2. Summary of sorting algorithms.

Program Name	Run Time in Microseconds	Time for sort of size N		
		100	1000	10,000
I1	$6.00N^2$	.06 sec	6.0 sec	10.0 min
I2	$3.90N^2$	.04 sec	3.9 sec	6.5 min
I3	$2.73N^2$	.03 sec	2.7 sec	4.5 min
I4	$2.02N^2$	.02 sec	2.0 sec	3.3 min
N1	$18N \log_2 N + 220N$	.034 sec	.40 sec	4.6 sec
N2	$16N \log_2 N + 220N$	.034 sec	.38 sec	4.3 sec
N3	$12N \log_2 N + 220N$	.030 sec	.34 sec	3.8 sec
N4	$12N \log_2 N$	.008 sec	.12 sec	1.6 sec
Sedgewick's	$8N \log_2 N$	.005 sec	.08 sec	1.1 sec

Table 8.3 describes the programs for searching. The format of the table is similar to that of Table 8.2. The times in that table denote the time for one million searches in a table of N elements, for $N = 100$, 1000, and 10,000.

Table 8.3. Summary of searching algorithms.

Program Name	Run Time in Microseconds	Time for 10^6 searches of size N		
		100	1000	10,000
D1	$3.65N$	6 min	1 hr	10 hr
D2	$2.05N$	3.5 min	33 min	5.5 hr
O1	$256 \log_2 N$	28 min	42 min	57 min
O2	$101 \log_2 N$	11 min	16.5 min	22 min
O3	$23 \log_2 N$	2.5 min	3.8 min	5 min
O4	$16 \log_2 N$	1.7 min	2.7 min	3.5 min
O5	$15 \log_2 N$	1.6 min	2.5 min	3.3 min
O6	$5 \log_2 N$	30 sec	50 sec	1.1 min
Steele's	$0.9 \log_2 N$	6 sec	9 sec	12 sec

The first lesson to be learned from these examples is the effect of changing the intramodular structure. In both problems, using sophisticated algorithms resulted in programs that were more subtle and had larger constants than their simpler cousins (the constants were originally much larger and were then squeezed to be comparable to those of the simpler algorithms). The sizes of those constants were very important for small values of N: the fast insertion sort was superior to the first `Quicksort` when N was 100, and the fast sequential search was superior to the first binary search even when N was 1000. As N increases, though, the asymptotically faster algorithms are bound to win in the end: the superiority is clear in both problems when N is 10,000.

The next lesson of the tables is the power of writing efficient code. The tables describe four distinct programs to which the method was applied; the constant factors squeezed from the programs (when $N = 1000$) were 1.8, 3, 5, and 51. The speedup achieved by this approach is fundamentally different than that achieved by changing algorithms: in most cases we increased one constant factor that will yield the same speedup for all values of N, whereas by changing algorithms we achieve more of a speedup as N increases. Increasing the speed by this method did result in longer and more subtle code.

To achieve the most efficient binary search program, Guy Steele worked at the lower design level of translation to machine code; by doing so he achieved another speedup of a factor of 5.5. He attained the efficient assembly code by using a high-quality compiler; had that tool not been available, he could have coded the same program by hand. Working at the two design levels of writing efficient code and translation to machine code led to an overall speedup in the binary search program of a factor of more than 280.

One of the most important tools we used in this chapter is too often neglected by programmers: the literature search. Most programmers are clever people who enjoy solving problems; when faced with an important problem, they would rather solve it themselves than see how someone else already did it. Indeed, that is one of the tasks that this book is meant to prepare the reader to accomplish. But such (admittedly fun) creativity must be supplemented by trips to a technical library, or at least your bookshelf, to see how others before you have solved the problem. Every practicing programmer should have some familiarity with an algorithms text such as those mentioned in Section 3.2; these books almost always provide insight for a particular problem, and sometimes even provide code that is straightforward to implement (as Aho, Hopcroft, and Ullman [1974] did for the two problems of this chapter). When a programmer is faced with a problem of writing efficient code, then he should of course immediately refer to this book; Appendix C is designed to help the programmer choose the most appropriate rule to apply in a given context. The best kind of reference to find, though, is one that addresses the immediate problem the programmer faces: for both of the problems in this chapter, the wise programmer would have referred immediately to Knuth [1973]. Studying others' approaches to the problem can give one both the immediate tools to solve the given problem and a chance to learn some tricks of the trade from a fellow craftsman.

8.4 EXERCISES

8.1. In this chapter we concentrated our attention on two primary algorithms for each problem: sequential and binary search, and insertion sort and `Quicksort`. The purpose of this exercise is to consider other algorithms for the two problems. The specific assignment is to implement a different algorithm as a Pascal (or other high-level language) program as a solution to the instances of the sorting and searching problems described in this chapter.

a. **Sorting.** Consider especially Shell sort, heap sort, and merge sort.

b. **Searching.** Consider Fibonaccian search and hashing (for hashing, we must slightly change the problem definition and allow the data structure to use extra space).

Knuth [1973] is a good reference for the above algorithms and data structures.

8.2. In this chapter we chose the algorithms and fine-tuned the programs to be efficient for problems of size $N = 1000$. Do the same for the sorting and searching problems when they are typically used on problems of size $N = 10$ and $N = 100$.

8.3. The Pascal modifications of this chapter will be effective across a variety of systems; use the system-dependent techniques of Chapter 6 to tune the programs to be efficient for a particular system.

8.4. [For assembly language programmers only.] Recode the inner loops of the programs in assembly code, and measure the running times of the resulting programs. How do their times compare to the high-level language programs?

8.5. The binary search of Fragment O6 is specialized to sorted tables of 1000 `real` numbers. Suppose that in a given system we wanted to perform very efficient binary searches on several (say, twenty) different sorted tables of `real`s of varying sizes. Discuss how we can achieve the time efficiency of Fragment O6 without sacrificing the space to unroll the loop of each procedure. (You may want to use some low-level constructs that are typically available only in assembly languages and system implementation languages such as Bliss and C.)

8.6. General-purpose tools are often the most efficient; this fact was discussed in Procedure Rule 2 (Exploit Common Cases) as the "Inventor's Paradox". Sometimes, though, exploiting special facts about a particular problem can both increase speed and decrease programming efforts. Sketch programs for solving the following special cases of the general problems (both special cases are idealized versions of problems that arose in real systems).

a. **Sorting.** Write a program to sort a set of $N \leq 27{,}000$ integers. Your program must read the input from a disk file and write the output to a different disk file; it may not use more than 2000 16-bit words of space (beyond that used for storing the code and disk buffers). Each integer is between 1 and 27,000; it is a fatal error condition if an integer occurs more than once in the set.

b. **Searching.** Store a set of 6000 (A,B) pairs in a 16-bit machine. The A's are distinct integers between 1 and 9999; the B's are integers between 1 and 200. The set is stored once; subsequently, many searches are performed. Each search is given an A value and must return the corresponding B value if it exists; if no such A value is in the set, then the search should return 0. Give two programs: the first should be optimized for speed, and the second should be optimized for space.

EPILOGUE

In the Preface of this book we set out to solve the problem of producing efficient software systems. Although we considered a number of design levels at which efficiency may be achieved, we have concentrated on the level of writing efficient code. In summary, we should take a moment to consider what all the work we have seen means to practicing programmers.

To do this, let's first let our minds wander to how things would be in the best of all possible worlds, and consider how efficiency would be faced by several interested parties.

- **System Designers.** As we saw in Section 1.2, the overall system design often determines the efficiency of the resulting systems; some designs could never yield efficient systems, while with others one would have to work to avoid efficiency. In the best of all possible worlds, the system designer would have automated tools such as those described by Smith [1981] to predict the performance of a design early in its life. Such tools will give us two benefits: we will be led away early from systems that would be impossible to implement efficiently, and we will learn the critical modules of any system we do implement.

- **Programmers.** In the best of all worlds, programmers will not worry often about efficiency. Because designers will use the tools mentioned above, programmers will be given only feasible systems to implement, and they will know the efficiency-critical modules if there are any. The primary approach to efficiency used by most programmers will be the proper choice of algorithms and data structures in the critical modules; they will be aided in that choice by well-documented software libraries. On the few occasions when programmers do have to use the techniques of writing efficient code, they will be assisted by program development systems that can help them maintain correctness while increasing the speed of the system.

- **Efficiency Experts.** When the system designers and programmers become stumped on an efficiency problem, they will be able to consult an efficiency expert (Sauer and Chandy [1981] and Smith [1981] refer to this expert as a "performance analyst" and a "performance engineer", respectively). Such an expert is an experienced software engineer familiar with tools for achieving efficiency at all the design levels of Section 1.2 and will be able to choose the right tool to apply in any particular context. Furthermore, he knows the literature well and is in professional contact with colleagues whom he can consult when he needs additional help.

- **Compiler Writers.** Our compiler in the best of all possible worlds will be a joy to use. It will support a language that makes system development relatively easy, and the code that it produces will be of the same quality that excellent assembly coders produce by hand. When the compiler knows that efficiency matters (which it will learn from the analysis of the overall system), it will learn from the analysis which resources are scarce and apply automated versions of many of the rules in this book to conserve them. On the few occasions when the programmer has to apply the techniques, the system will assist him by presenting profiles and gathering statistics on the efficiency of various approaches.

Lofty views of the heavens give us a vision, but after such respites most of us have to get back in the trenches and continue slugging it out. Although we do not live in the best of all possible worlds, many of the notions we just considered can be manifested in most environments.

- **System Designers.** Even though designers cannot immediately use automated tools to analyze the performance of an unimplemented system, Smith's [1980, 1981] methodology can be applied by hand to give much information. That information can perform the two functions mentioned above: steer us away from impractical designs, and identify the critical modules in solid designs. Such estimates should be used by system designers whenever efficiency could conceivably become an issue in the life of the system (which is almost always).

- **Programmers.** The good news for programmers is that they should rarely worry about efficiency. Using the methodology of Section 3.3, they can ignore the issue of efficiency in most systems, and only consider it when it really does matter. In many of those cases, the right tool to solve their efficiency problem is the field of algorithms and data structures. In some cases, though, they will have to resort to wringing efficiency out of the system by writing efficient code; the purpose of this book is to help them to do that in as orderly a way as possible.

- **Efficiency Experts.** Although I have yet to meet a person with this job title, I know of many shops that do indeed have resident efficiency experts. Such experts come in two flavors: someone who knows a particular system inside and out is handy, but a person who knows the programmer's craft and can see to the heart of a computational problem is invaluable. If you know such an expert, take your efficiency problems to him after you try to solve them yourself; you will usually get a better solution, and each of you will learn something from the other. If you are this expert in your shop, congratulations: you are in a good position to learn from your colleagues as you help them. Continue to earn the respect of your colleagues by continuing to grow professionally; you must read the right journals and books to keep up. And if you happen to be in the fortunate position of having such an expert work for you, encourage him in his important role as a consultant, teacher, and student.

- **Compiler Writers.** It is truly sad that although there are many good compilers currently on the market, many programmers have to work in assembly code if they don't want to give up a time factor of two or three right off the bat. Managers owe it to their troops to equip them with good tools; the excuses for not doing so that held water in the mid 1970's have now passed away. If there is one dominant message in this book for compiler writers, it is a plea to include profiling in all systems; it is foolish to spend so much of your effort dealing with the problem of efficiency, and then not give the applications programmer the simple tools to let him do his end of the job.

The above discussion wanders from the core of this book, which is writing efficient code. I would like to return to that subject for a final admonition. The techniques of writing efficient code are in many ways like a snakebite kit: used in the right context, they can be just the thing for the job at hand, but their inappropriate application can be disastrous. Unfortunately, most programmers like to play with new toys. I have many friends who, immediately upon buying a snakebite kit, would be tempted to throw the first person they see to the ground, tie the tourniquet on him, slash him with the knife, and apply suction to the wound. What that action does to people, you might be tempted to do to software systems by haphazardly applying the techniques of this book. Please don't. Study these rules to learn better your craft as a programmer, and then use them when they are needed.

APPENDIX A

DETAILS OF THE
PASCAL PROGRAMS

In Chapter 2 we studied a sequence of Pascal code fragments for producing Nearest Neighbor Traveling Salesman Tours. This appendix contains some details about the Pascal programs that contained those fragments. The experiments were conducted in early September, 1980. The compiler used for these experiments was the system Pascal compiler on the Carnegie-Mellon University Computer Science Department PDP-KL10 (Arpanet Host CMUA), which is a derivative of the Hamburg Pascal compiler. It performs little optimization, so the computation we see expressed in the source code closely models the resulting object code. All tests were run with the array bounds checking and debugging features turned off.

In Chapter 2 we assigned a running time to each fragment of the form K_1N^2 microseconds. Such a time is, of course, merely an approximation; the actual run time of Fragments A1 through A5 is actually of the form

$$K_1N^2 + K_2NH_N + K_3N + o(N),$$

while for Fragments A6 through A9 the run time appears to have the form

$$K_1N^2 + K_2N^{3/2} + o(N^{3/2}).$$

Because it would be laborious and not terribly instructive to calculate all the values of the various K's, we will use instead the simple approximation to K_1 of dividing the total run time in microseconds by N^2. Table A.1 shows the run times of several experiments; the rows represent the nine fragments and the columns represent values of N from 100 to 1000. Each entry consists of the average run time in seconds placed above the 95 percent confidence interval for the run time in seconds, which is in turn placed above the estimated value of K_1.

Table A.1. Pascal program run times.

Program #	100	200	N 400	800	1000
1	.4845 (.0075) 48.4	1.8786 (.0060) 47.0			
2	.4533 (.0047) 45.3	1.8249 (.0044) 45.6			
3	.2392 (.0046) 23.9	.9707 (.0030) 24.2			
4	.2118 (.0035) 21.2	.8465 (.0033) 21.2			
5	.1425 (.0051) 14.25	.5578 (.0034) 13.94	2.2241 (.0166) 14.01		
6	.0945 (.0047) 9.45	.3614 (.0049) 9.04	1.3857 (.0036) 8.66	5.3332 (.0179) 8.33	8.2456 (.0159) 8.25
7	.1066 (.0024) 10.66	.3683 (.0021) 9.21	1.3160 (.0058) 8.22	4.9034 (.0125) 7.66	7.5268 (.0113) 7.53
8	.1036 (.0047) 10.36	.3418 (.0040) 8.54	1.2153 (.0041) 7.60	4.5094 (.0081) 7.05	6.9334 (.0139) 6.93
9	.1033 (.0026) 10.33	.3431 (.0041) 8.58	1.2068 (.0047) 7.54	4.4330 (.0077) 6.93	6.7936 (.0081) 6.79

Table A.1 is ragged due to the expense of using Fragments A1 through A5 on inputs of size greater than 200; recall that Fragment A1 requires approximately 47 seconds on a 1000-point set. Each program was run on ten different data sets uniformly distributed on the unit square $[0,1]^2$ for the point sets with 100, 200, and 400 points; on the 800- and 1000-point sets each program was run on five different data sets. The small values of the 95% confidence intervals give us confidence that any statistical error in the table occurs in at most the third digit of the reported times.

Because the above data is only for one compiler on one machine architecture, we might be worried that our estimates of the coefficient K_1 are more artifacts of the particular system than values inherent in the underlying programs. To test this, William J. Trosky transliterated Fragments A1 through A8 from Pascal to C and performed experiments identical to those described above using the C compiler on a Hewlett-Packard HP-1000 computing system. His results are summarized in Table A.2; the first column gives the program number, the second column gives the estimate of the coefficient K_1 for the Pascal program (in microseconds), and the third column normalizes that coefficient by dividing it by the coefficient for Fragment A6; the fourth and fifth columns give the corresponding values for the C program. It is satisfying to note that the normalized run times of the Pascal and C programs are remarkably similar. (A C version of Fragment A9 was not available.)

Table A.2. Comparison of run times.

Program #	Pascal Programs Coefficient	C Programs Normalized	Coefficient	Normalized
1	47.0	5.73	311.8	4.39
2	45.6	5.56	303.8	4.27
3	24.2	2.95	197.4	2.78
4	21.2	2.59	187.2	2.63
5	14.0	1.71	122.0	1.72
6	8.2	1	71.1	1
7	7.5	.91	61.1	.86
8	6.9	.84	59.8	.84
9	6.8	.83	—	—

Table A.3 presents data on the number of minimal values of `CloseDist` found by Fragments A1 through A9 (the transformations do not change the expected number of minima). The first column gives N, the number of points in the sets. Tests were run on ten point sets for values of N up to 400, and on five point sets for larger values of N. The second column shows the average number of observed new minima in the point sets, and the next column gives the ninety-five percent confidence interval of that value. The fourth column divides the third column by N; our analysis predicts that to be the sum of the first N harmonic numbers divided by N, or approximately $H_N - 1$, which is shown in the final column. The last two columns show that the observed values were close to the predicted values.

Table A.3. Data on new minima.

N	New Minima	(95% Conf.)	New/N	$H_N - 1$
4	2.4	(.34)	.60	1.083
9	13.4	(1.58)	1.49	1.829
16	36.4	(4.37)	2.28	2.381
25	64.9	(6.37)	2.60	2.816
36	104.2	(8.88)	2.89	3.175
49	161.8	(9.75)	3.30	3.479
64	232.1	(16.47)	3.63	3.744
81	313.4	(13.90)	4.12	3.978
100	422.1	(34.12)	4.22	4.187
144	628.4	(46.96)	4.36	4.550
196	915.3	(47.44)	4.67	4.858
256	1296.6	(64.19)	5.06	5.124
324	1790.2	(92.07)	5.53	5.360
400	2230.1	(90.88)	5.57	5.570
484	2764.4	(136.01)	5.71	5.760
576	3443.4	(148.02)	5.98	5.934
676	4133.2	(316.78)	6.11	6.094
784	4791.4	(180.01)	6.11	6.242
900	5677.4	(237.42)	6.31	6.380

Table A.4 presents data on the efficacy of delaying computing the y-distance in Fragment A6. The first column gives N, the number of points, the second column gives the average number of total y-values calculated during the execution of the program, and the third column gives the 95% confidence interval of the second column. These statistics were gathered on the same point sets used for the statistics of Table A.3. The fourth and fifth columns show the average number of y-distances divided by N and $N^{3/2}$, respectively. The fifth column indicates that the total number of y-distances is on the average less than $1.5N^{3/2}$. This fact implies that when M points are left unvisited, $2.25M^{1/2}$ y-distances are calculated on the average (because the sum over all values of M from 1 to N of that value is approximately $1.5N^{3/2}$).

Table A.4. Data on y-values tested.

N	Raw	(95% Conf.)	Raw/N	Raw/$N^{3/2}$
4	5.7	(.55)	1.425	.7125
9	27.6	(2.16)	3.033	1.011
16	80.4	(4.58)	5.025	1.256
25	148.5	(4.54)	5.940	1.188
36	268.9	(11.57)	7.469	1.245
49	440.4	(18.73)	8.988	1.284
64	697.5	(21.33)	10.898	1.362
81	978.1	(28.64)	12.075	1.342
100	1347.8	(61.38)	13.478	1.348
144	2368.1	(89.55)	16.445	1.370
196	3753.9	(121.94)	19.153	1.368
256	5666.5	(181.51)	22.135	1.383
324	8462.4	(216.93)	26.119	1.451
400	11150.0	(355.52)	27.875	1.394
484	15016.4	(354.65)	31.026	1.410
576	19619.0	(622.45)	34.061	1.419
676	25196.2	(778.70)	37.272	1.434
784	31452.6	(1205.47)	40.118	1.433
900	38365.0	(676.01)	42.628	1.421

APPENDIX B

ASSEMBLY PROGRAMS FOR
THE TRAVELING
SALESMAN PROBLEM

In this appendix we will see how the speed of the assembly code Fragment A10 of Section 2.3 can be increased by applying the techniques of Chapters 4 and 5. Although we will study the problem in the assembly language of the IBM System/360-370 computer, the purpose of this chapter is not to illustrate coding tricks on that particular system. Rather, this appendix has the following two purposes:

- To show that the techniques of Chapters 4 and 5 can be applied to assembly language programs.
- To illustrate the benefits of applying those techniques to assembly language programs; we will see that the speed of the carefully coded Fragment A10 can be increased by a factor of almost four.

To assign costs to the various program fragments, we will use the cost model described by Knuth [1971, p. 116].

Each instruction costs one unit, plus one if it fetches or stores an operand from memory or if it is a branch that is taken, plus a penalty for specific lower opcodes:

Floating add/subtract	add 1
Multiply	add 5
Divide	add 8
Multiply double	add 13
Shift	add 1
Load multiple	add $n/2$ (n registers loaded)
Store multiple	add $n/3$ (n registers stored)

This evaluation corresponds roughly to 1 unit per 0.7 microseconds on our [IBM System/360] model 67 computer.

Knuth also assumed that the square root function requires 85 units. He pointed out that the details of the above model can vary from machine to machine, but these costs are roughly applicable for a broad class of machines.

As a review, the inner loop of Fragment A10 is repeated below. To the right of each instruction is noted its cost in Knuth's units. Because the inner loop has a total cost of 13 time units and that loop is executed $\sim N^2/2$ times, the dominant term of the entire program's cost will be $6.5N^2$ time units. The BH (Branch High) instruction is assigned cost 2 because it will be taken all but $O(M^{1/2})$ times when M points remain.

```
Loop     LA    I,8(I)                  1
         L     ThisDist,0(I)           2
         SR    ThisDist,ThisX          1
         MR    ThisDist,ThisDist       6
         CR    ThisDist,CloseDist      1
         BH    Loop                    2
```

Fragment A10.   Inner loop of Fragment A10.

It is easy to see that most of the time of the above code is spent in the multiply instruction. We can reduce that cost by replacing the square with an absolute value, but this requires that CloseDist contain the square root of its previous value, as it did in Fragments A1 and A2. This change can be viewed as an application of Logic Rule 1 or Expression Rule 2 (Exploit Algebraic Identities). (Recall that we considered a similar change when studying Fragment A6, but it decreased the speed of the Pascal program—thus this change is system dependent.) The 8 time units of the resulting inner loop imply a running time of $\sim 4.0N^2$ units for Fragment A11.

```
Loop     LA    I,8(I)                  1
         L     ThisDist,0(I)           2
         SR    ThisDist,ThisX          1
         LPR   ThisDist,ThisDist       1
         CR    ThisDist,CloseDist      1
         BH    Loop                    2
```

Fragment A11.   Replace multiply with absolute value.

The previous change makes the purpose of this loop somewhat clearer: it is looking for all values within a certain range, when most values are outside that range. In the above fragment we represent the range by its center and its radius; we will again use Logic Rule 2 and Expression Rule 2 (Exploit Algebraic Identities) to change the representation of the range. Specifically, we will initialize the register HiLimit to contain the maximum value in the range, and register `LoLimit` to contain one less than the minimum value in the range. (The reason for this asymmetric representation will become clear in Fragment A13.) The resulting code is shown in Fragment A12; the cost of 7.0 units in the inner loop implies a run time of $3.5N^2$ time units.

```
Loop    LA    I,8(I)              1
        L     ThisDist,0(I)       2
        CR    ThisDist,HiLimit    1
        BH    Loop                1.5
        CR    ThisDist,LoLimit    0.5
        BLE   Loop                1
```

Fragment A12. Replace multiply with absolute value.

The BH instruction has the cost 1.5 because it is always executed and the branch is taken half the time, on the average, because the current element is equally likely to be above the range as below it.[1] The second CR instruction is then executed half the times, while the BLE instruction is executed half the times but is almost always taken.

The bulk of the work of Fragment A12 is going to two pairs of instructions that successively perform a comparison and then a conditional branch. When Guy Steele [1981] inspected this fragment, he immediately observed this fact and tried to find some way to combine each pair into a single instruction. (He was using a microscopic application of Procedure Rule 5—Parallelism.) Even though he had never programmed the IBM System/360, he knew that most machines have loop instructions that perform both a comparison and a branch, and in a few minutes he looked up the BXH (Branch on Index High) and BXLE (Branch on Index Less than or Equal) in the System/360 assembly language description. This resulted in the code of Fragment A13, whose 5.5 units in the inner loop give a $\sim 2.75N^2$ overall running time.

```
Loop    LA    I,8(I)                    1
        L     ThisDist,0(I)             2
        BXH   ThisDist,HiPair,Loop      1.5
        BXLE  ThisDist,LoPair,Loop      1
```

Fragment A11. Replace multiply with absolute value.

In the above fragment, `HiPair` is an even register that contains zero (which is added to `ThisDist` before the sum is compared with the upper bound of the range); the next register is `HiLimit` of the previous fragment. Similarly,

---

[1] For the reader not comfortable with merely assuming this, we could instead use a randomizing program that tosses a coin before going through the inner loop to choose randomly whether it will first test the upper or lower bound of the range; the program would then conditionally branch to one of two inner loops.

`LoPair` is an even register that contains zero and the next register is `LoLimit`.

The two comparisons now account for 2.5 units each iteration of the loop, while the overhead of incrementing `I` and loading `ThisDist` require 3 units; we will therefore focus on reducing that overhead. The LA instruction can be easily removed by Loop Rule 3—Loop Unrolling. Unrolling the loop k times reduces its cost per loop to $2/k$ time units; this cost can be made as small as desired. This results in Fragment A14, with a run time of $\sim 2.25N^2$ units; because that fragment is so similar to Fragment A13, it will not be shown.

Besides the BXH and BXLE instructions, the only instruction remaining in the inner loop is the L instruction that loads the current value into a register. The cost of that instruction can be reduced by an application of Procedure Rule 5 (Parallelism): the System/360 has the LM instruction that can load a sequence of m words from memory into m consecutive registers at a cost of $1 + m/2$ units. If we use this instruction to load seven consecutive elements of `IntArr` into registers, we can load four desired x-values with a cost of just 4.5 units, for a per-element cost of just 1.125 time units (we load only seven elements because the System/360 has just sixteen general-purpose registers, and many of those are already used for other tasks in this program). This results in a total cost for the inner loop of 3.625 time units, which gives a program run time of $\sim 1.8125N^2$ time units for Fragment A15. (Note that a slight reorganization of the data structure to separate the x- and y-values into two arrays would allow more x-values to be loaded and thereby reduce the per-element load cost to approximately 0.5 units, which would decrease the time of the entire program to approximately $1.57N^2$ time units.)

APPENDIX C

SUMMARY OF THE RULES

The following list restates each rule from Chapters 4 and 5 and then briefly summarizes the major points made in the text. A list of the names of the rules can be found in Section 7.2 on page 110.

SPACE-FOR-TIME RULES

Space-For-Time Rule 1—Data Structure Augmentation: The time required for common operations on data can often be reduced by augmenting the structure with extra information or by changing the information within the structure so that it can be accessed more easily. (Page 39.)

- Reference counters facilitate garbage collection by keeping additional information in dynamically allocated nodes.
- Hints augment data structures by keeping a fast but possibly inaccurate structure along with a slow but robust structure.

Space-For-Time Rule 2—Store Precomputed Results: The cost of recomputing an expensive function can be reduced by computing the function only once and storing the results. Subsequent requests for the function are then handled by table lookup rather than by computing the function. (Page 40.)

- Peterson stored the value of evaluated board positions to reduce the time of a game playing program from 27.10 seconds to 0.18 seconds.
- A procedure for computing Fibonacci numbers can be replaced by a table of the numbers.

- Stu Feldman precomputed the number of ones in all eight-bit strings to reduce run time from over a week to less than two hours.

Space-For-Time Rule 3—Caching: Data that is accessed most often should be the cheapest to access. (Page 42.)

- Jalics found that caching the last element retrieved from a table reduced the access cost from 2004 instructions to 4 instructions in 99% of the queries.
- Chris Van Wyk's storage allocator cached the most popular kind of node and reduced the system run time by over fifty percent; Peter Deutsch cached activation records in an allocator and reduced run time by thirty percent.
- In implementing a dictionary, keep most of the dictionary on disk but cache the most common words in core.
- Rick Cattell cached recently-used tuples in a database system to reduce the time of an access from 8 milliseconds to 1.4 milliseconds.
- Caching can "backfire" and increase the run time of a program if locality is not present in the underlying data.

Space-For-Time Rule 4—Lazy Evaluation: The strategy of never evaluating an item until it is needed avoids evaluations of unnecessary items. (Page 43.)

- In building a table of Fibonacci numbers, only compute the numbers actually used.
- Al Aho evaluated the elements of a table as they were needed and reduced the run time of a program from 30 seconds to less than half a second.
- Brian Kernighan reduced the run time of a document formatter by twenty percent by calculating the width of the current line only as needed rather than for every input character.

TIME-FOR-SPACE RULES

Time-For-Space Rule 1—Packing: Dense storage representations can decrease storage costs by increasing the time required to store and retrieve data. (Page 45.)

- Storing integers in one decimal digit per eight-bit byte, two digits per byte, and in binary format represent three levels of packing.
- The space of a database system could be reduced by one-third by packing three integers (between 0 and 1000) in two 16-bit words.
- John Laird reduced the time required to read a file of real numbers by a factor of over 80 by packing the file.
- Stu Feldman found that by *unpacking* a table he increased the data space slightly but decreased the code space by over four thousand words.
- *Overlaying* reduces data space by storing data items that are never simultaneously active in the same memory space.

- Code overlaying reduces code space by using the same storage for routines that are never simultaneously needed. Many operating systems provide this service automatically in their virtual memory systems.

Time-For-Space Rule 2—Interpreters: The space required to represent a program can often be decreased by the use of interpreters in which common sequences of operations are represented compactly. (Page 47.)

- Finite State Machines (FSM's) can be implemented by small tables; they are easy to define, code, prove correct, and maintain.
- Brooks describes how an interpreter led to small space requirements for a console interpreter, and how the time spent in decoding a dense representation of a FORTRAN compiler was paid for by drastically reduced input and output costs.
- In some systems the programmer should use the interpreter provided by the underlying machine architecture and "compile" common operations into machine code.

LOOP RULES

Loop Rule 1—Code Motion Out of Loops: Instead of performing a certain computation in each iteration of a loop, it is better to perform it only once, outside the loop. (Page 52.)

- Moving the calculation of a constant factor outside a `for` loop reduced its time from $138N$ microseconds to $7.9N$ microseconds.
- Code cannot be moved out of loops if it has side effects that are desired on every iteration.

Loop Rule 2—Combining Tests: An efficient inner loop should contain as few tests as possible, and preferably only one. The programmer should therefore try to simulate some of the exit conditions of the loop by other exit conditions. (Page 53.)

- Adding a sentinel in the last element of an unsorted vector reduced the time to search it from $7.3C$ to $4.1C$ microseconds.
- Sentinels can decrease the robustness of a program. Improper use of a sentinel caused a C compiler to generate non-reentrant code; the bug surfaced rarely, but was fatal in those circumstances.
- *Sentinels* are a common application of Loop Rule 2: we place a sentinel at the boundary of a data structure to reduce the cost of testing whether our search has exhausted the structure.
- Bob Sproull described how the lexical analyzer of the SAIL compiler used a control character at the end of the input buffer as a sentinel to avoid testing for end-of-buffer on each input character.

- Combining tests in the sequential search of a sorted array *increased* the run time from 6.8C microseconds to 7.3C microseconds (due to a system-dependent peculiarity); using sentinels finally reduced the search time to 4.1C microseconds.

- Bob Sproull described how three tests could be combined into one to increase the speed of the inner loop of a screen editor.

Loop Rule 3—Loop Unrolling: A large cost of some short loops is in modifying the loop indices. That cost can often be reduced by unrolling the loop. (Page 56.)

- Unrolling a loop to sum an array of ten real numbers reduced the run time from 63.4 microseconds to 22.1 microseconds.

- Unrolling the loop of a sequential search reduced its time from 4.1C microseconds to 3.4C microseconds.

Loop Rule 4—Transfer-Driven Loop Unrolling: If a large cost of an inner loop is devoted to trivial assignments, then those assignments can often be removed by repeating the code and changing the use of variables. Specifically, to remove the assignment I: =J, the subsequent code must treat J as though it were I. (Page 59.)

- Unrolling the inner loop of a routine for Fibonacci numbers reduced its time from 273 microseconds to 143 microseconds.

- Knuth used unrolling to decrease the time of inserting an element into a linked list by 16 percent.

Loop Rule 5—Unconditional Branch Removal: A fast loop should contain no unconditional branches. An unconditional branch at the end of a loop can be removed by "rotating" the loop to have a conditional branch at the bottom. (Page 62.)

- This technique is applicable only in low-level languages.

Loop Rule 6—Loop Fusion: If two nearby loops operate on the same set of elements, then combine their operational parts and use only one set of loop control operations. (Page 63.)

- To find the maximum and minimum elements in an array, we make only one iterative pass through the array.

LOGIC RULES

Logic Rule 1—Exploit Algebraic Identities: If the evaluation of a logical expression is costly, replace it by an algebraically equivalent expression that is cheaper to evaluate. (Page 66.)

- Simple optimizations are often done by compilers; programmers must be careful that a change of this type does not result in slower code.

- An algebraic identity allowed us to remove the square root in Fragment A2 to yield Fragment A3; this gave a speedup of almost a factor of two.

Logic Rule 2—Short-circuiting Monotone Functions: If we wish to test whether some monotone nondecreasing function of several variables is over a certain threshold, then we need not evaluate any of the variables once the threshold has been reached. (Page 67.)

- A simple application is evaluating and and or: to evaluate A and B we need not test B if A is false.
- Short-circuiting the distance evaluation in Fragment A5 reduced the time of Fragment A6 by forty percent.
- A more complex application of this rule exits from a loop as soon as the purpose of the loop has been accomplished.

Logic Rule 3—Reordering Tests: Logical tests should be arranged such that inexpensive and often successful tests precede expensive and rarely successful tests. (Page 69.)

- This was used in testing the character types in a lexical analyzer.
- This rule is used to push an expensive test inside a cheaper test.
- Peter Weinberger used a single-line test in a Scrabble program that was able to avoid an expensive test in over 99% of the cases.

Logic Rule 4—Precompute Logical Functions: A logical function over a small finite domain can be replaced by a lookup in a table that represents the domain. (Page 72.)

- Testing character types in a lexical analyzer is often implemented by a table of character types indexed by characters; Brian Kernighan reports that this reduced the run time of some programs by thirty to forty percent.
- David Moon designed a fast interpreter for a PDP-8 that had one table entry for each of the 4096 possible instructions.

Logic Rule 5—Boolean Variable Elimination: We can remove boolean variables from a program by replacing the assignment to a boolean variable V by an if-then-else statement in which one branch represents the case that V is true and the other represents the case that V is false. (This generalizes to case statements and other logical control structures.) (Page 73.)

- This rule usually decreases time slightly (say, less than 25 percent), but greatly increases code space.
- More complex applications of this rule remove boolean variables from data structures by keeping separate structures for the true and false records.

PROCEDURE RULES

Procedure Rule 1—Collapsing Procedure Hierarchies: The run times of the elements of a set of procedures that (nonrecursively) call themselves can often be reduced by rewriting procedures in line and binding the passed variables. (Page 75.)

- Rewriting the distance procedure in line reduced the run time of Fragment A4 from $21.2N^2$ microseconds to $14.0N^2$ microseconds.
- Dennis Ritchie increased the speed of a macro processor by a factor of four by writing procedures in line.

Procedure Rule 2—Exploit Common Cases: Procedures should be organized to handle all cases correctly and common cases efficiently. (Page 76.)

- Mary Shaw used this technique to increase the efficiency of the register SAVE and UNSAVE operations on the Rice University Computer; efficiently handling the special case of operating on all possible registers reduced the run time of some programs by thirty percent.
- This rule encourages us to remove unneeded generality from subroutines; Chris Van Wyk increased the speed of a program by a factor of three by using a special-purpose procedure for intersecting line segments.
- We should organize systems so that efficient cases are common cases; by ensuring that bit fields always start in the same positions in words, Rob Pike increased the efficiency of a raster graphics operation by a factor of two.

Procedure Rule 3—Coroutines: A multiple-pass algorithm can often be turned into a single-pass algorithm by use of coroutines. (Page 79.)

- An intermediate file that is written sequentially and then read sequentially can often be removed by linking together the two programs as coroutines; this increases space requirements but reduces costly input/output operations.

Procedure Rule 4—Transformations on Recursive Procedures: The run time of recursive procedures can often be reduced by applying the following transformations: (Page 80.)

- Code the recursion explicitly by use of a program stack.
- If the final action of a procedure P is to call itself recursively, replace that call by a goto to its first statement; this is usually known as removing tail recursion. That goto can often be transformed into a loop.
- If a procedure contains only one recursive call on itself, then it is not necessary to store the return address on the stack.
- It is often more efficient to solve small subproblems by use of an auxiliary procedure, rather than by recurring down to problems of size zero or one.

Procedure Rule 5—Parallelism: A program should be structured to exploit as much of the parallelism as possible in the underlying hardware. (Page 80.)

- Kulsrud, Sedgewick, Smith, and Szymanski used techniques at many design levels to build a Quicksort program on a Cray-1 that can sort 800,000 elements in less than 1.5 seconds.

EXPRESSION RULES

Expression Rule 1—Compile-Time Initialization: As many variables as possible should be initialized before program execution. (Page 82.)

- John Laird preprocessed data unchanged between runs of a program to reduce the program's run time from 120 seconds to 4 seconds.

Expression Rule 2—Exploit Algebraic Identities: If the evaluation of an expression is costly, replace it by an algebraically equivalent expression that is cheaper to evaluate. (Page 82.)

- An algebraic identity yields a fast range test that compiler writers can use on two's-complement architectures.
- We can often multiply or divide by powers of two by shifting left or right.
- Strength reduction on a loop that iterates through the elements of an array replaces a multiplication by an addition. This technique generalizes to a large class of incremental algorithms.
- David Jefferson used an incremental algorithm to reduce the number of characters sent to a terminal by a factor of over five.

Expression Rule 3—Common Subexpression Elimination: If the same expression is evaluated twice with none of its variables altered between evaluations, then the second evaluation can be avoided by storing the result of the first and using that in place of the second. (Page 84.)

- We cannot eliminate the common evaluation of an expression with important side-effects.

Expression Rule 4—Pairing Computation: If two similar expressions are frequently evaluated together, then we should make a new procedure that evaluates them as a pair. (Page 84.)

- Knuth reported that both the sine and the cosine of a given angle can be computed together for 1.5 times the cost of computing either individually. Similarly, the maximum and the minimum elements of a vector can be found at about 1.5 times the cost of finding either one.

Expression Rule 5—Exploit Word Parallelism: Use the full word width of the underlying computer architecture to evaluate expensive expressions. (Page 85.)

- When we OR two 32-bit sets together giving as output their 32-bit union, we are performing 32 operations in parallel.
- Stu Feldman's program to count one bits in a word (described in Space-For-Time Rule 1) and Peter Weinberger's Scrabble program (described in Logic Rule 3) both use this rule.

APPENDIX D

THE PASCAL DIALECT

This appendix is a brief introduction to the Pascal dialect used throughout this book. The first part contains a complete Pascal program; its purpose is to illustrate the structure of a Pascal routine. The second part is a glossary of the Pascal constructs used in the book. These two parts should help most readers understand enough Pascal to read the examples in this book; the reader interested in more details about the language should consult Jensen and Wirth [1975].

We will first study the following complete Pascal program. It performs no useful function; its purpose is to illustrate the general form of a Pascal program and its subroutines. The line numbers are not part of the input file; they are used for reference below.

```
01   program        Example(output);
02   const          Max = 10;
03   type           ArrPtr = 1..Max;
04                  RealPair = record X,Y: real end;
05   var            I,N: ArrPtr;
06                  A: array [ArrPtr] of RealPair;
07
08   procedure SetRanges(L,U:ArrPtr; Master: real);
09          var I: ArrPtr;
10          begin
11          for I := L to U do
12                  begin
13                  A[I].X := Master;
14                  A[I].Y := Master
15                  end
16          end;
17
18   procedure Swap(var X,Y: real);
19          var T: real;
20          begin
21          T := X; X := Y; Y := T
22          end;
23
24   begin
25   N := 5;
26   SetRanges(1,N,1.0);
27   SetRanges(3,N,2.0);
28   Swap(A[1].X, A[N].Y);
29   for I := 1 to N do
30   writeln(output, A[I].X, A[I].Y)
31   end.
```

When the above program is executed, it produces the following output on the default output file output (which is usually either the user's terminal or a line printer).

```
2.0000000      1.0000000
1.0000000      1.0000000
2.0000000      2.0000000
2.0000000      2.0000000
2.0000000      1.0000000
```

There are six main parts in the above program that are typical of the Pascal programs throughout this book. The following list briefly summarizes the parts; we will study them in detail shortly.

- The program statement. This statement names the program and lists the files the program uses. This statement is not present in the fragments in the text because they are not complete programs.

- Constant declarations. Following the keyword `const` is a list of compile-time constants and their values.
- Type declarations. Following the keyword `type` is a list of program-specific type declarations. The types defined here may be used later in the program whenever a type is needed; these augment the built-in types provided by the language.
- Variable declarations. Following the keyword `var` is a list of variables in the program and the type of each variable.
- Procedures and functions. The next part of the program is a list of procedures and functions. Each of the procedures and functions has the same form as the overall program; they consist of the procedure or function header, constant declarations, type declarations, variables, subprocedures and subfunctions, followed finally by the program statements. Some of those parts may be absent.
- Main program. The final part of the program is the sequence of statements that is the main program, enclosed in `begin-end` statements.

We will now examine the parts of the program in detail.

Line 1 names the program and tells the files it uses; this is the header of the program unit. Procedures and functions also have headers: they name their routines and describe their parameters.

Line 2 is a declaration of constants; it says that whenever the name `Max` appears in the source text, the integer `10` is to be substituted. The string `Max` does not denote a program variable; it is merely an informative way of writing the constant `10`.

Lines 3 and 4 declare new program types. The type `ArrPtr` is declared to be an integer in the range from 1 to `Max`, which is in this case `10`. A variable can now be declared to be of type `ArrPtr`, and can assume any integer between 1 and 10. The type `RealPair` is defined to be a record that consists of a pair of real numbers named X and Y.

Lines 5 and 6 declare the variables of the program. Both I and N are variables of type `ArrPtr`; they can contain integer variables between 1 and 10. The variable A is an array of elements. Each element is of type `RealPair`, so each element contains both X and Y components. The elements are indexed by a variable of type `ArrPtr` (an integer from 1 to 10), so there are a total of 10 elements of the array. The first element is `A[1]`; it has the two real components `A[1].X` and `A[1].Y`.

Lines 8 through 16 define a new procedure named `SetRanges`. Its purpose is to set both components of all records from `A[L]` to `A[U]` to the real value `Master`. The procedure has three input parameters: L and U are both of type `ArrPtr` (that is, an integer between 1 and 10), and `Master` is of type `real`. The procedure declares one local variable: it is named I and it is of type

`ArrPtr`. (It could also declare constants or types, if needed.) The final part of
the procedure is the executable code, which is straightforward.

The next procedure is named `Swap`. It has the effect of exchanging its
two input parameters, which are both real numbers. Because the procedure
modifies its parameters, they must be declared as `var` parameters. The procedure declares one local variable named T of type `real`; the operation of the
procedure is straightforward.

Lines 24 through 31 are the main body of the program. The statement in
Line 25 sets the variable N to be 5 (which is an integer in the valid range
`1..10`). Line 26 sets both the X and Y components of all elements of
`A[1..5]` to be equal to the real number `1.0`. The next statement sets both the
X and Y components of all elements of `A[3..5]` to the real `2.0`. Line 28
swaps the X component of record `A[1]` (which is `1.0`) with the Y component
of record `A[5]` (which is `2.0`). Lines 29 and 30 then print both the X and Y
components of the records `A[1]` through `A[5]`.

The following is a brief, informal glossary of the Pascal terms used in this
book; it should not be construed as a definition of Pascal. Some Pascal constructs are used throughout this book only in limited forms; this glossary defines
those terms only in those limited forms and ignores their more general uses in
Standard Pascal. This book also uses several constructs that are not part of Standard Pascal but are present in many Pascal implementations; those constructs are
marked accordingly. Several constructs that are used in only one place in the
book are described in a footnote when they are used, and are not included in this
glossary.

`array`   A one-dimensional array is a variable defined as
                 "`array [Type1] of Type2`"; in that declaration
                 `Type1` is a range (such as `1..10` or `L..U`, where L and U
                 are defined in a `const` statement), and `Type2` is any type.

Arithmetic operations
                 The operation `div` denotes integer division; A `div` B
                 returns the integer quotient of A divided by B (for instance, 7
                 `div` 2 is 3). The real functions `sqr` and `sqrt` return the
                 square and square root of their real arguments, respectively.
                 The `boolean` function `odd` returns `true` if its integer input
                 is odd and `false` if its input is even. The `real` function
                 `exp(X)` returns e^X, where $e = 2.7182818284590....$ The
                 function `trunc(X)` (where X is a nonnegative real number)
                 returns the greatest integer less than or equal to X, while
                 `round(X)` returns the integer closest to X.

Assignment   The statement X `:=` Y sets the variable X to the value of
                 the expression Y.

`begin-end`   Enclosing a sequence of statements separated by semi-colons
                 ("`;`") within the Pascal key words `begin` and `end` allows

the sequence of statements to be treated as a single statement. Because loops and conditional statements are defined in Pascal as consisting of Pascal statements, begin-end blocks are commonly used in those constructs. (This corresponds roughly to the PL/1 DO-END statements.)

break

See loop-endloop.

Comments

Text enclosed between the delimiters "(*" and "*)" is a comment not processed by the compiler.

Comparison operators

The standard operators $<$, $=$, and $>$ denote "less than", "equal to", and "greater than", respectively. "Not greater than" and "not less than" are denoted by $<=$ and $>=$, respectively. "Not equal to" is denoted by $<>$.

const

The constant declaration "const Max=10;" creates the constant Max that has the value 10 (which cannot be changed at run time). The subscript type in an array declaration is usually declared with constants of this form; this practice leads to programs that are easier to modify than programs in which the constants appear in every array definition.

for-do

The statement "for I := L to U do S" executes the statement S with the variable I successively taking on the values L, L+1, ..., U.

function-return

[**Not Standard Pascal.**] The declaration "function F(A,B,C: Type1): Type2;" says that F is a function of the three variables A, B, and C of type Type1 and returns a value of type Type2. A function can be used wherever an expression is legal; evaluation of the function transfers control to the subroutine, and the statement return X causes control to return to the caller with the value X. (The return statement is not Standard Pascal; it was used in this book because it is similar to constructs in other languages.)

goto

[**Not Standard Pascal.**] The statement "goto X" causes control to transfer to the statement labelled X. Standard Pascal allows only numeric labels that must be declared in a procedure header; this book allows undeclared variable names as labels.

if-then-else

The statement "if E then S_1 else S_2" first evaluates the boolean expression E. If E is true, then S_1 is executed, otherwise S_2 is executed. If no else clause is specified and E is false, then no action is taken.

Input-output statements

The statement read(A,B,C) reads the values of the variables A, B, and C from the input file; the statement readln(A,B,C) does the same and additionally reads all characters until a line terminator is found. The statement write(A,B,C) writes A, B, and C onto the output file; the statement writeln(A,B,C) additionally writes a line terminator (which causes subsequent output to appear on a new line).

Logical operators **[Not Standard Pascal.]** The expression "not A" returns true if and only if the boolean expression A is false. The expression "A or B" is true if and only if at least one of A and B is true; the expression "A and B" is true if and only if both A and B are true. The expression "A cor B" has the same value as "A or B", but B is not evaluated if A is true; similarly, "A cand B" has the same value as "A and B", but B is not evaluated if A is false. (The cand and cor operators are not Standard Pascal.)

loop-endloop **[Not Standard Pascal.]** The statement "loop S endloop" causes the series of statements S to be executed repeatedly until one of the statements of S executes a break statement.

procedure The declaration "procedure F(A,B,C: Type1);" says that the procedure F is passed the three parameters A, B and C. The procedure can be called by writing the statement F(D,E,F) wherever a statement is valid.

repeat-until The statement "repeat S until B" repeatedly executes the series of statements S and evaluates the boolean condition B until B is true. The series S is always executed at least once.

record A record is a Pascal type that allows a user to treat related information as a unit. For instance, the statement

        type ExampleRecord = record
                I: integer; X: real end;

defines a new type named ExampleRecord that has the two components named I and X. If we later have the statement

        var R: ExampleRecord;

then R is a variable of type ExampleRecord; we could refer to R's integer component by R.I and to R's real component by R.X.

Types Pascal provides several intrinsic data types: boolean variables are either true or false, char variables contain a single character, integer variables contain an integer from some system-dependent range, and real variables contain real numbers (over a system-dependent range to a system-dependent accuracy).   Additionally, programmers can use type statements to define new types; common types are integer ranges (such as Min..Max) and records.

var

The var statement in a program or routine header specifies that a list of program variables follows. In the parameter list of a procedure, a var statement denotes a variable that can be modified by the procedure.

while-do

The statement "while B do S" repeatedly tests the boolean condition B and executes statement S if B is true; this process terminates as soon as B is false. If B is false the first time it is tested, then the statement S is never executed.

REFERENCES

AHO, A. V. [1980].   Private communication of A. V. Aho of Bell Telephone Laboratories, Murray Hill, NJ, December 1980.

AHO, A. V., J. E. HOPCROFT, and J. D. ULLMAN [1974]. *The Design and Analysis of Computer Algorithms*, Addison-Wesley, Reading, MA.

AHO, A. V. and J. D. ULLMAN [1977]. *Principles of Compiler Design*, Addison-Wesley, Reading, MA.

AUSLANDER, M. A. and H. R. STRONG [1978]. "Systematic recursion removal", *Communications of the ACM 21*, 2, February 1978, pp. 127-134.

BAASE, S. [1978]. *Computer Algorithms: Introduction to Design and Analysis*, Addison-Wesley, Reading, MA.

BASKETT, F. [1978]. "The best simple code generation techniques for WHILE, FOR and DO loops", *SIGPlan Notices 13*, 4, April 1978, pp. 31-32.

BEELER, M., R. W. GOSPER, and R. SCHROEPPEL [1972]. HAKMEM, Artificial Intelligence Memo No. 239, Massachusetts Institute of Technology, February 1972.

BENTLEY, J. L. [1979]. "An introduction to algorithm design", *IEEE Computer Magazine 12*, 2, February 1979, pp. 66-78.

BENTLEY, J. L., M. G. FAUST, and F. P. PREPARATA [1982]. "Approximation algorithms for convex hulls", *Communications of the ACM 25*, 1, January 1982, pp. 64-68.

BENTLEY, J. L. and J. H. FRIEDMAN [1979]. "Data structures for range searching", *Computing Surveys 11*, 4, December 1979, pp. 397-409.

BENTLEY, J. L. and J. B. SAXE [1980]. "An analysis of two heuristics for the euclidean travelling salesman problem", *Eighteenth Annual Allerton Conference on Communication, Control and Computing*, October 1980, pp. 41-49, University of Illinois Coordinated Science Laboratory.

BERGERON, R. D. and H. R. BULTERMAN [1975]. "A technique for evaluation of user systems on an IBM S/370", *Software—Practice and Experience 5*, 1, January-March 1975, pp. 83-92.

BIRD, R. S. [1980]. "Tabulation techniques for recursive programs", *Computing Surveys 12*, 4, December 1980, pp. 403-417.

BOYER, R. S. and J S. MOORE [1977]. "A fast string searching algorithm", *Communications of the ACM 20*, 10, October 1977, pp. 762-772.

BRAILSFORD, D. F., E. FOXLEY, K. C. MANDER, and D. J. MORGAN [1979]. "Run-time profiling of Algol 68-R programs using DIDYMUS and SCAMP", *SIGPlan Notices 12*, 6, June 1977, pp. 27-35.

BROOKS, F. P., Jr. [1975]. *The Mythical Man Month: Essays in Software Engineering*, Addison-Wesley, Reading, MA.

BURSTALL, R. M. and J. DARLINGTON [1977]. "A transformation system for developing recursive programs", *Journal of the ACM 24*, 1, January 1977, pp. 44-67.

CATTELL, R. G. [1981]. Private communication of R. G. Cattell of Xerox Palo Alto Research Center, Palo Alto, CA, May 1981.

CONWAY, R. W. and D. GRIES [1976]. *Primer on Structured Programming Using PL/I, PL/C, and PL/CT*, Winthrop, Cambridge, MA.

DARLINGTON, J. and R. M. BURSTALL [1976]. "A system which automatically improves programs", *Acta Informatica 6*, 1, pp. 41-60.

DEUTSCH, L. P. [1981]. Private communication of L. P. Deutsch of Xerox Palo Alto Research Center, Palo Alto, CA, August 1981.

DONGARRA, J. J. and A. R. HINDS [1979]. "Unrolling loops in FORTRAN", *Software—Practice and Experience 9*, 3, March 1979, pp. 219-226.

FEIGN, D. [1980]. "Programming tricks of last resort for desperados: an investigation into the advantages of assembly language coding". Ph.D. Thesis, University of California at Irvine. Available from University Microfilms International, Ann Arbor, Michigan, and London.

FELDMAN, S. [1981]. Private communication of S. Feldman of Bell Telephone Laboratories, Murray Hill, NJ, July 1981.

FINKEL, R. A. [1981]. Private communication of R. A. Finkel of the University of Wisconsin, Madison, WI, June 1981.

FITCH, G. P. [1977]. "Profiling a large program", *Software—Practice and Experience 7*, 4, July-August 1977, pp. 511-518.

FRIEDMAN, J. H., J. L. BENTLEY, and R. A. FINKEL [1977]. "An algorithm for finding best matches in logarithmic expected time", *ACM Transactions on Mathematical Software 3*, 3, September 1977, pp. 209-226.

FULLER, S. H. and F. BASKETT [1975]. "An analysis of drum storage units", *Journal of the ACM 22*, 1, January 1975, pp. 83-105.

GARDNER, M. [1970]. "Mathematical games", *Scientific American 223*, 4, October 1970, pp. 120-123.

GOODMAN, S. E. and S. T. HEDETNIEMI [1977]. *Introduction to the Design and Analysis of Algorithms*, McGraw-Hill, New York, NY.

GOSLING, J. A. [1981]. Private communication of J. A. Gosling of Carnegie-Mellon University, Pittsburgh, PA, June 1981.

GUNTHER, F. J. [1981]. "Programming for speed", *Computers and Programming 21*, 5, September/October 1981, pp. 65, 68.

HEINDEL, L. E. and P. W. PURDOM, Jr. [1967]. "The automatic optimization of SLIP routines", *SIGSAM Bulletin*, Number 8, December 1967, pp. 21-30.

HOROWITZ, E. and S. SAHNI [1978]. *Fundamentals of Computer Algorithms*, Computer Science Press, Inc., Rockville, MD.

JACKSON, M. A. [1975]. *Principles of Program Design*, Academic Press, New York, NY.

JALICS, P. J. [1977]. "Improving performance the easy way", *Datamation 23*, 4, April 1977, pp. 135-148.

JEFFERSON, D. R. [1981]. Private communication of D. R. Jefferson of the University of Southern California, Los Angeles, CA, November 1981.

JENSEN, K. and N. WIRTH [1975]. *Pascal User Manual and Report*, Second Edition, Springer Verlag, New York, NY.

JOHNSON, S. C. [1981]. Private communication of S. C. Johnson of Bell Telephone Laboratories, Murray Hill, NJ, July 1981.

KERNIGHAN, B. W. [1981]. Private communication of B. W. Kernighan of Bell Telephone Laboratories, Murray Hill, NJ, February through November, 1981.

KERNIGHAN, B. W. and P. J. PLAUGER [1976]. *Software Tools*, Addison-Wesley, Reading, MA.

KERNIGHAN, B. W. and P. J. PLAUGER [1978]. *The Elements of Programming Style*, Second Edition, McGraw-Hill, New York, NY.

KNUTH, D. E. [1968]. *The Art of Computer Programming, volume 1: Fundamental Algorithms*, Addison-Wesley, Reading, MA.

KNUTH, D. E. [1969]. *The Art of Computer Programming, volume 2: Seminumerical Algorithms*, Addison-Wesley, Reading, MA.

KNUTH, D. E. [1971]. "An empirical study of FORTRAN programs", *Software—Practice and Experience 1*, 2, April-June 1971, pp. 105-133.

KNUTH, D. E. [1973]. *The Art of Computer Programming, volume 3: Sorting and Searching*, Addison-Wesley, Reading, MA.

KNUTH, D. E. [1974]. "Structured programming with **goto** statements", *Computing Surveys 6*, 4, December 1974, pp. 261-301.

KREITZBERG, C. S. and B. SHNEIDERMAN [1972]. *The Elements of FORTRAN Style: Techniques for Effective Programming*, Harcourt Brace Jovanovich, New York, NY.

KULSRUD, H. E., R. SEDGEWICK, P. SMITH, and T. G. SZYMANSKI [1978]. Partition sorting on CRAY-1, SCAMP Working Paper No. 7/78, Institute for Defense Analyses, Princeton, NJ, September 1978.

LAIRD, J. E. [1981]. Private communication of J. E. Laird of Carnegie-Mellon University, Pittsburgh, PA, March 1981.

LAMPSON, B. W. and R. F. SPROULL [1979]. "An open operating system for a single-user machine", *Proceedings of the Seventh Symposium on Operating Systems* Principles, December 1979, pp. 98-105, ACM.

LEVERETT, B. [1977]. Performance Evaluation of High-Level Language Systems, Carnegie-Mellon University Computer Science Technical Report, November 1977, 39 pp.

LEWIS, H. and C. H. PAPADIMITRIOU [1978]. "The efficiency of algorithms", *Scientific American 238*, 1, January 1978, pp. 96-109.

LEWIS, J. [1979]. "Low-level program optimization: Some illustrative cases", *BYTE 4*, 10, October 1979, pp. 168-172. (Reprinted in Liffick [1979].)

LIFFICK, B. W., ed. [1979]. *Programming Techniques, volume 4: Bits and Pieces*, BYTE Books, McGraw-Hill, New York, NY.

LOVEMAN, D. B. [1977]. "Program improvement by source-to-source transformation", *Journal of the ACM 24*, 1, January 1974, pp. 121-145.

MATWIN, S. and M. MISSALA [1976]. "A simple, machine independent tool for obtaining rough measures of Pascal programs", *SIGPlan Notices 11*, 8, August 1976, pp. 42-45.

McCRACKEN, D. D. [1957]. *Digital Computer Programming*, John Wiley and Sons, New York, NY.

McFARLAND, M. C. [1981]. Mathematical models for formal verification in a design automation system, unpublished Ph.D. Thesis, Department of Electrical Engineering, Carnegie-Mellon University, July 1981.

McILROY, M. D. [1981]. Private communication of M. D. McIlroy of Bell Telephone Laboratories, Murray Hill, NJ, July 1981.

McKELLAR, A. C. and E. G. COFFMAN, Jr. [1969]. "Organizing matrices and matrix operations for paged memory systems", *Communications of the ACM 12*, 3, March 1969, pp. 153-165.

McNAIR, T. J. (ed.) [1972]. *Hamilton Bailey's Emergency Surgery*, Ninth Edition, John Wright and Sons, Ltd., Bristol, Great Britian (distributed in the U.S.A. by The Williams and Wilkins Company, Baltimore, MD).

MONT-REYNAUD, B. [1976]. Removing trivial assignments from programs, Stanford

University Computer Science Department Report STAN-CS-76-544, Stanford, California, March 1976.

MOON, D. A. [1981]. Private communication of D. A. Moon of the Massachusetts Institute of Technology, Cambridge, MA, March 1981.

MORRIS, R. [1978]. "Counting large numbers of events in small registers", *Communications of the ACM 21*, 10, October 1978, pp. 840-842.

NELSON, B. J. [1981]. Remote Procedure Call, Ph.D. Thesis, Carnegie-Mellon University, Computer Science Report CMU-CS-81-119, May 1981.

NEUHOLD, E. J. and H. W. LAWSON, JR. [1971]. *The PL/I Machine: An Introduction to Programming*, Addison-Wesley, Reading, MA.

NEWELL, A. [1981]. Private communication of A. Newell of Carnegie-Mellon University, Pittsburgh, PA, March 1981.

NIX, R. [1981]. "Experience with a space efficient way to store a dictionary", *Communications of the ACM 24*, 5, May 1981, pp. 297-298.

NOYCE, W. B. [1978]. "Optimization: A case study", *BYTE 3*, 4, April 1978, pp. 40-45. (Reprinted in Liffick [1979].)

PAIGE, R. [1979]. Expression Continuity and the Formal Differentiation of Algorithms, Courant Computer Science Report Number 15, September 1979.

PETERSON, J. L. [1975]. A Programming Methodology (Preliminary Version), Unpublished technical report, University of Texas at Austin, 13 pp.

PETERSON, J. L. [1979]. "Text compression", *BYTE 4*, 12, December 1979, pp. 106-118. (Reprinted in Liffick [1979].)

PETERSON, J. L. [1980]. *Computer Programs for Spelling Correction: An Experiment in Program Design*, Springer-Verlag, New York, NY.

PETERSON, J. L. [1981]. Private communication of J. L. Peterson of the University of Texas, Austin, TX, June 1981.

PIKE, R. [1981]. Private communication of R. Pike of Bell Telephone Laboratories, Murray Hill, NJ, July 1981.

PLATTNER, B. and J. NIEVERGELT [1981]. "Monitoring program execution: A survey", *IEEE Computer Magazine 14*, 11, November 1981, pp. 76-93.

POLYA, G. [1945]. *How To Solve It*, Princeton University Press, Princeton, NJ.

REDDY, D. R. and A. NEWELL [1977]. "Multiplicative speedup of systems", in *Perspectives on Computer Science*, A. K. Jones (ed.), pp. 183-198, Academic Press, New York, NY.

REGHBATI, H. K. [1981]. "An overview of data compression techniques", *IEEE Computer Magazine 14*, 4, April 1981, pp. 71-75.

REID, B. K. [1980]. Scribe: A Document Specification Language and Its Compiler, Ph.D. Thesis, Department of Computer Science, Carnegie-Mellon University, September 1980. (See also Reid and Walker [1980].)

REID, B. K. and J. H. WALKER [1980]. *Scribe User's Manual, Third Edition*, published by Unilogic, Ltd., 160 N. Craig Street, Pittsburgh, PA, 15213.

REINGOLD, E. M., J. NIEVERGELT, and N. DEO [1977]. *Combinatorial Algorithms: Theory and Practice*, Prentice-Hall, Englewood Cliffs, NJ.

RITCHIE, D. M. and K. THOMPSON [1978]. "The UNIX time-sharing system", *Bell System Technical Journal 57*, 6, pp. 1905-1930, July-August 1978. (An earlier version is in *Communications of the ACM 17*, 7, pp. 365-375, July 1974.)

RUSSELL, R. D. [1978]. "The PDP-11: A case study of how *not* to design condition codes", *Proceedings of the Fifth Annual Symposium on Computer Architecture*, pp. 190-194, IEEE and ACM.

SATTERTHWAITE, E. H. [1972]. "Debugging tools for high level languages", *Software—Practice and Experience 2*, 3, July-September 1972, pp. 197-217.

SAUER, C. H. and K. M. CHANDY [1981]. *Computer Systems Performance Modeling*, Prentice-Hall, Englewood Cliffs, NJ.

SCHAEFER, M. [1973]. *A Mathematical Theory of Global Program Optimization*, Prentice-Hall, Englewood Cliffs, NJ.

SCHEIFLER, R. W. [1977]. "An analysis of inline substitution for a structured programming language", *Communications of the ACM 20*, 9, September 1977, pp. 647-654.

SCHERLIS, W. L. [1980]. Expression Procedures and Program Derivation, Ph.D. Thesis, Stanford Computer Science Report STAN-CS-80-818, Stanford, CA, August 1980.

SEDGEWICK, R. [1975]. Quicksort, Ph.D. Thesis, Stanford Computer Science Report STAN-CS-75-492, Stanford, CA, May 1975.

SEDGEWICK, R. [1978]. "Implementing Quicksort programs", *Communications of the ACM 21*, 10, October 1978, pp. 847-857.

SHAW, M. [1979]. A Formal System for Specifying and Verifying Program Performance, Carnegie-Mellon University Computer Science Technical Report CMU-CS-79-129, June 1979. (A preliminary version of the material in this report can be found in Wulf, Shaw, Hilfinger and Flon [1981, Section 6.5].)

SHAW, M. and W. A. WULF [1980]. "Toward relaxing assumptions in languages and their implementations", *SIGPlan Notices 15*, 3, March 1980, pp. 45-61.

SITES, R. L. [1978]. "Programming tools: Statement counts and procedure timings", *SIGPlan Notices 13*, 12, December 1978, pp. 98-101.

SMITH, C. U. [1978]. "Methods for improving the performance of applications programs", *Computer Measurement Group Transactions 22*, December 1978.

SMITH, C. U. [1980]. "Consider the performance of large software systems before implementations", *Proceedings of the Computer Measurement Group 11*, Boston, MA, December 1980.

SMITH, C. U. [1981]. "Increasing information systems productivity by software performance engineering", Duke University Computer Science Department Technical Report CS-1981-3, May 1981.

SPROULL, R. F. [1981a]. "Using program transformations to derive line-drawing algorithms", Carnegie-Mellon University Computer Science Technical Report CMU-CS-81-117, April 1981.

Sproull R. F. [1981b]. Private communication of R. F. Sproull of CARNEGIE-MELLON UNIVERSITY, May 1981.

STANAT, D. F. [1981]. Private communication of D. F. Stanat of the University of North Carolina, Chapel Hill, NC, November 1981.

STANDISH, T. A. [1980]. *Data Structure Techniques*, Addison-Wesley, Reading, MA.

STANDISH, T. A., D. C. HARRIMAN, D. F. KIBLER, and J. M. NEIGHBORS [1976]. The Irvine Program Transformation Catalog, Technical Report, Department of Information and Computer Science, University of California at Irvine.

STANKOVICH, J. A. [1979]. Structured Systems and Their Performance Improvement Through Vertical Migration, Technical Report No. CS-41, Department of Computer Science, Brown University, May 1979.

STEELE, G. L., JR. [1977a]. "Debunking the 'expensive procedure call' myth", *Proceedings of the ACM National Conference '77*, October 1977, pp. 153-162.

STEELE, G. L., JR. [1977b]. "Arithmetic shifting considered harmful", *SIGPlan Notices 12*, 11, November 1977, pp. 61-69.

STEELE, G. L., JR. [1981]. Private communication of G. L. Steele Jr. of Carnegie-Mellon University, Pittsburgh, PA, April 1981.

VAN WYK, C. J. [1981]. Private communications of C. J. Van Wyk of Bell Telephone Laboratories, Murray Hill, NJ, December 1980 through July 1981.

VYSSOTSKY, V. A. [1976]. What I'd Like Computer Science To Tell Me, unpublished internal memorandum, Bell Telephone Laboratories, Murray Hill, NJ, May 18, 1976, 12 pp.

VYSSOTSKY, V. A. [1981]. Private communication of V. A. Vyssotsky of Bell Telephone Laboratories, Murray Hill, NJ, July 1981.

WAITE, W. M. [1974]. "Code generation", in *Compiler Construction: An Advanced Course*, F. L. Bauer and J. Erckel (eds.), pp. 549-602, Springer-Verlag, New York, NY.

WALDBAUM, G. [1978]. Tuning Computer Users' Programs, IBM Computer Science Research Report RJ-2409, IBM Research Laboratory, San Jose, CA, December 4, 1978, 37 pp.

WEINBERG, G. M. [1971]. *The Psychology of Computer Programming*, Van Nostrand Reinhold Company, New York, NY.

WEINBERGER, P. J. [1981]. Private communication of P. J. Weinberger of Bell Telephone Laboratories, Murray Hill, NJ, July 1981.

WICHMAN, B. A. [1976]. "Ackermann's function: A study in the efficiency of calling procedures", *BIT 16*, 1, pp. 103-110.

WULF, W. A. [1981].   Private communication of W. A. Wulf of Carnegie-Mellon University, Pittsburgh, PA, April 1981.

WULF, W. A., R. K. JOHNSSON, C. B. WEINSTOCK, S. O. HOBBS, and C. M. GESCHKE [1975]. *Design of an Optimizing Compiler*, American Elsevier Publishing Company, Inc., New York, NY.

WULF, W. A., M. SHAW, P. N. HILFINGER, and L. FLON [1981].   *Fundamental Structures of Computer Science*, Addison-Wesley, Reading, MA.

INDEX